Sunset

W9-BLB-488

Reinvent Your Kids' Rooms

DISCOVER

By Christine E. Barnes and the Editors of Sunset Books

MENLO PARK · CALIFORNIA

SUNSET BOOKS

VICE PRESIDENT, GENERAL MANAGER: Richard A. Smeby

VICE PRESIDENT, EDITORIAL DIRECTOR: Bob Doyle

PRODUCTION DIRECTOR: Lory Day

DIRECTOR OPERATIONS: Rosann Sutherland

ART DIRECTOR: Vasken Guiragossian

STAFF FOR THIS BOOK

DEVELOPMENTAL EDITOR: Linda J. Selden

PROJECT DESIGNERS: Melinda D. Douros, Heidi M. Emmett, D. Kimberly Smith, and Debra S. Weiss

COPY EDITOR AND INDEXER: Julie Harris

PHOTO DIRECTOR/STYLIST: JoAnn Masaoka Van Atta

DESIGN: Dorothy Marschall/Marschall Design

PAGE PRODUCTION: Maureen Spuhler

ILLUSTRATOR: Beverley Bozarth Colgan

PRINCIPAL PHOTOGRAPHER: E. Andrew McKinney

PREPRESS COORDINATOR: Danielle Javier

PROOFREADER: Mary Roybal

10 9 8 7 6 5 4 3 2 1

ISBN 0–376–01793–7
Library of Congress Control Number: 2002100918
Printed in the United States of America

For additional copies of *Reinvent Your Kids' Rooms* or any other Sunset book, call 1–800–526–5111 or see our web site at *www.sunsetbooks.com*

COVER: An attic bedroom becomes a sweet retreat, complete with puffy duvet cover, lacy stenciled walls, and a window treatment inspired by a vintage coat hanger.
INTERIOR DESIGN: Christine E. Barnes, Heidi M. Emmett, Dale Miller, D. Kimberly Smith, and Debra S. Weiss
PHOTOGRAPHY: E. Andrew McKinney
COVER DESIGN: Vasken Guiragossian
PHOTO DIRECTION: JoAnn Masaoka Van Atta

DESIGN CREDITS

Christine E. Barnes: 10, 14, 28, 52, 102

Melinda D. Douros: 82, 95, 98, 106, 110, 128, 130, 140, 143

Heidi M. Emmett: 25, 39, 44, 47, 63, 66, 70, 71, 74, 77, 79, 87, 94, 118, 144

Dale Miller: 29

D. Kimberly Smith/Deer Creek Design: 20, 35, 79, 90, 95, 98, 106, 124, 128, 136, 140, 142, 143

Debra S. Weiss: 22, 32, 47, 60, 63, 70, 71, 87, 115, 118

When it's time to change the look of our kids' rooms, most of us don't think "remodel," or even "redecorate." Children's rooms require an approach that adapts what we have and adds new furnishings and features as budgets allow. Hand in hand with this approach is a fresh attitude—think of it as the "reinvent spirit."

This spirit calls for a sense of adventure, a willingness to consider every aspect of your child's room. The six kids' rooms on the following pages are total packages—new wall color, soft furnishings, storage, and furniture, along with quick-and-easy ideas. Although the effects are dramatic, these major changes are easy to achieve because the steps are simple and the supplies are readily available. If a complete makeover isn't in your plans right now, you can still give your child's room a lift with one or more of the projects and ideas shown in this book.

Reinvention also includes the satisfaction that comes from personal effort. Work hard, but enjoy the process and take pleasure in making your child's room something special.

We would like to thank the following individuals and firms for their expertise and assistance: Bay View Tile, Dunn-Edwards Paints, Andrew J. Sellery, Sierra Tile & Stone, Sarah Weiss, and Young's Carpet One. Thanks also to the homeowners who graciously invited us into their busy lives: Dale and Gary Miller and Susan and Greg Straub.

Contents

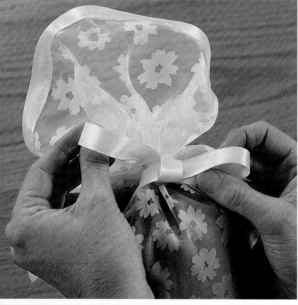

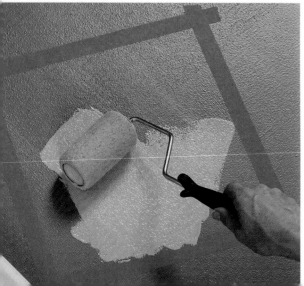

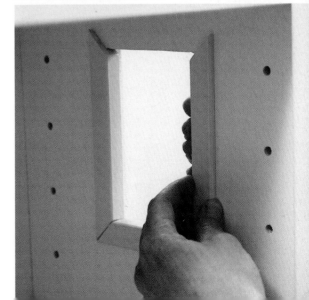

Room for Change

A room is a memorable part of every child's life. It's a personal space for play, sleep, study, reading, and just hanging out, as well as a reflection of current interests. As chil-

dren grow, those interests change, making their rooms ideally suited to reinvention. ∾ Deciding to reinvent your child's room is easy; knowing where to begin may not be. Take a cue from the pros

Sweet Retreat describes this old-fashioned attic hideaway

and start by analyzing the room "as is." Focus first on what to keep—recently installed flooring, for example, or a bed

frame your child still likes—and make a list of these givens. ∾ Then, sit down with your child and look at the rooms and projects on the following pages. You'll see six distinct styles: sweet and old-

Shared Space is twice as nice for sisters

fashioned; artistic and airy; casual and cozy; high-tech and futuristic; rustic and bold; pretty and pastel. Formulate a wish list

of existing features you can reinvent, as well as brand-new projects you'd like to make. In this book you'll find a variety of techniques, including deco-rative paint, sewing, stenciling, and simple wood-

Denim Days are carefree and casual in an upstairs bonus room

working. Many of the projects

6

shown will work in more than one style of room, making it easy to pull together a totally original look. Let your child pick the colors whenever possible, and resist the

urge to impose your preferences; kids need to feel that their rooms are *theirs.* ❧ Once you've set-tled on a reinvent plan, work from "the walls in" and "the floors up," as designers say, to create a backdrop and a foundation for subse-

Past, present, and future merge in the Outer Limits

quent projects. A number of features in this book help make the projects easy to fol-low. A colored tab at the start of each project tells you the approximate time commitment, such as "Do It Today" and "In a Weekend," or identify it as a special type of project, such as "Wood Shop" or "Sewing Workshop." Simple

It's all play and no work in these colorful Rustic Quarters

instructions, photographs, and illustrations guide you through the step-by-step process; tips sprinkled throughout keep you on track. In the "Fresh Ideas" sections, you'll see the finishing touches that make each room special. ❧ Ready to reinvent? Turn the page and take

a tour through these creative rooms.   A fresh palette sets the scene for Parfait Dreams

Sweet Retreat

WHEN A SPECIAL LITTLE GIRL goes to her grandmother's house to stay, a dreamy attic bedroom awaits her. A coat of true blue paint started the transformation; painting just the walls kept the project easy and economical. A puffy patchwork duvet cover looks cozy and inviting on the existing wrought-iron daybed, now with its brass finials painted white to blend with the fabrics. The real star here, however, is the charming "curtain rod" inspired by a vintage coat hanger, complete with painted-on logo and slogan. Diaphanous tulle panels flank the window and complement lacy designs stenciled on the walls.

White walls did nothing to highlight the sloped ceiling of this upstairs bedroom; a pleated shade at the window was strictly functional.

MATERIALS

²/₃ yard *each* of
six different fabrics
for pillow top

6- by 24-inch rotary
ruler with a 45-degree-
angle line, available
at fabric stores and
quilt shops

Fabric marker that
washes out

Pins

Walking-foot attachment

Thread to blend

5-inch scissors

1 yard of fabric
for pillow back

18-inch pillow form

NOTE: Fabrics must be
at least 40 inches
wide and all cotton.
Do not prewash fabrics.

SEWING WORKSHOP

Faux Chenille Pillow

FAUX CHENILLE IS SOFT, subtle, and irresistible to young fingers. To create the faux chenille pillow you see here, six different fabric squares were stacked and stitched together in V-shaped lines; then the layers were slashed between the stitched lines to create raw-edged rows that "bloom," or fluff out, when washed and dried. A walking foot for your sewing machine is essential to this project. If you don't already have one, inquire about the cost (before buying the fabric) because a walking foot can be expensive.

FINISHED SIZE

17 by 17 inches

Making and Stitching the Rows

THE SECRET TO SUCCESS WITH FAUX CHENILLE IS TO CHOOSE A FABRIC WITH A DEFINITE DESIGN FOR THE TOP LAYER. WHEN THE CHENILLE IS CREATED, THE EFFECT WILL BE A "GHOSTED" VERSION OF THE ORIGINAL DESIGN. VARY THE FABRICS FOR THE LAYERS UNDERNEATH, INCLUDING A MIX OF COLORS AND PATTERNS.

1 Decide which fabric will be the foundation (it will be the least visible in the finished pillow); cut it approximately 24 inches square. Cut each of the other fabrics approximately 22 inches square, making your cuts exactly straight.

2 On the right side of the fabric chosen for the top layer, measure and mark a vertical line down the center. Using this line as your reference, mark a 45-degree-angle line (shown in pink here) on either side of the center so the lines form a V. These are "base lines."

3 Above and below the lines, mark additional base lines at 6-inch increments. (The 6-inch-wide ruler makes this easy to do.) Check each line with the 45-degree-angle line on your ruler and the center line.

4 Above and below the base lines, mark lines at 1-inch increments, always measuring from a base line. Pin the center line, a few of the angled lines, and the outer edges, pinning through all layers.

5 With your walking foot attached and starting at the right edge, carefully stitch on the first base line you drew, up to the center line. Remove pins just before you reach them.

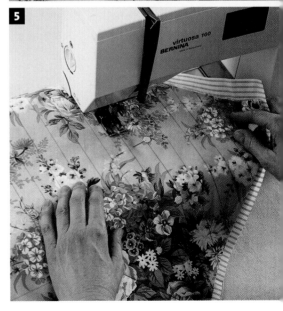

five layers of fabric but on top of the foundation (see photo 9a). Cut through the layers, being careful not to cut the foundation. (If you cut this layer, your pillow cover will have holes.) The tautness of the fabrics will naturally guide your scissors down the middle of the row (see photo 9b).

10 Carefully cut up to the center line—but not through it. Cut the remaining rows in the same way.

Assembling the Pillow

11 Trim the thread ends to prevent tangling. Wash your stitched piece in hot water with several towels

6 At the center line, leave the needle down, raise the presser foot, and pivot the fabrics so the walking foot is centered over the opposite angled line.

7 Continue stitching on the base line until you reach the other edge. Remove the layered fabrics, and trim the threads. Stitch the remaining lines in the same way, working first above the original base lines, then below them.

8 Now stitch between the stitched lines, using the stitching to center your walking foot. (Some walking-foot attachments are 1 inch wide, making it easy to center the foot between the stitching.)

9 Using your 5-inch scissors, slide the bottom blade between two stitched lines and under the first

or pairs of jeans and dry them on the "cotton" setting. Wash and dry the piece a second time to soften it even more.

12 Working on the back and using the center line as your reference, carefully measure and mark the stitched piece to 18 inches square. Cut on the marked lines.

13 Prewash your backing fabric. Measure, mark, and cut two pieces, each 18 by 12 inches. On one long edge of each piece, turn under ½ inch and press. Turn the raw edge in to meet the pressed fold and press again; pin. Hem each edge by machine.

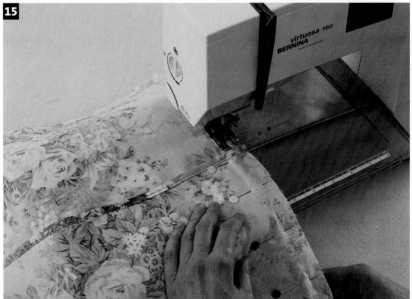

14 Lay the pillow top, right side up, on your work surface. Lay the backing pieces, right sides down, on the pillow top so the edges and corners are aligned and the hemmed edges overlap as shown. Pin the pieces together along the edges.

15 With your walking foot attached, stitch around the pillow top using a ½-inch seam allowance. Remove the pins just before you reach them.

16 Trim the edges ¼ inch from the stitching, trimming the corners at an angle to reduce bulk. Turn the pillow cover right side out and insert the form through the envelope closure.

Patchwork Duvet Cover

FLORAL PRINTS AND FLUFFY WHITE CHENILLE combine in this easy-to-make duvet cover based on an old-fashioned quilt design. Fabric choice is the key to making great patchwork blocks. For the larger squares in the blocks select a print with a fairly open background, such as the soft blue stripe shown here. For the smaller squares choose fabrics with enough contrast in color and pattern to read as separate shapes.

FINISHED SIZE

approximately
60 by 84 inches

14

Making the Patchwork Blocks

1 From each fabric for the smaller squares, cut six 12- by 15-inch pieces. Using one piece of each fabric, place their right sides together and press with your iron set on "cotton/ steam." Set aside the remaining pieces.

2 Trim ½ inch off a long edge of the paired fabrics using your rotary tools, cutting through both layers at once. Align the just-trimmed edge with the 3½-inch line on your rotary ruler and cut a layered pair of strips. Cut a second and third pair of strips, also 3½ inches wide. Each pair of strips will be used to make the two four-patch units in one block.

3 If your sewing machine doesn't have a mark for stitching a precise ¼-inch seam allowance, you can create a seam guide by layering strips of masking tape on the face-plate ¼ inch from the needle position. Pin the paired strips on one long edge. Stitch using a ¼-inch seam allowance. All the following seam allowances are also ¼ inch wide.

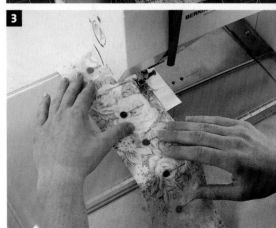

4 Lay the stitched strips on your pressing surface, with the darker strip on top. Gently fold back the top strip and press it flat against the seam allowances.

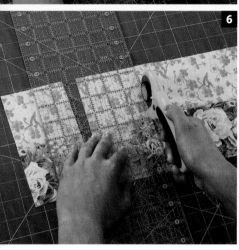

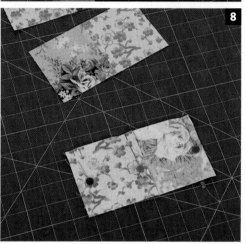

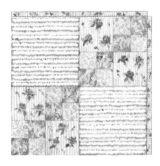

5 With the stitched strips right side up, trim the ragged end.

6 Crosscut four segments, each 3½ inches wide. Use the marks on your ruler to make sure the cuts are precisely perpendicular to the seam and the upper and lower raw edges. You don't want the segments to "lean" in either direction.

7 With right sides together and the prints alternating, butt the seam allowances of two segments. The seam allowances should face in opposite directions and fit snugly together.

8 Pin the segments together along one edge, placing a pin close to, but not through, the seam allowances. Also place a pin at each end. Stitch.

9 Open the top segment and press it flat against the seam allowances to complete one four-patch unit. Repeat Steps 7 and 8 to make a second four-patch unit; press flat.

10 From the fabric for the larger squares, cut 36 squares, each 6½ by 6½ inches.

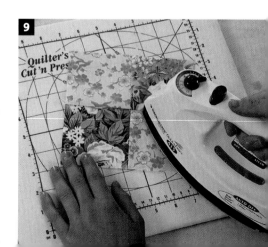

11 Lay out the four-patch units and the squares as shown. Make sure the four-patch units are arranged so the same fabric is toward the center.

12 With right sides together and raw edges aligned, pin the square and four-patch unit shown at the top in Step 11. Stitch, making sure the seam allowances on the four-patch unit stays flat underneath.

13 With the square on top, fold back the square and press it flat against the seam allowances. Pin and stitch the remaining square and four-patch unit; press flat.

14 Lay out the half-blocks with the fabrics alternating, as shown.

15 With right sides together and raw edges aligned, butt the seam allowances of the two half-blocks as you did in Step 7. Pin and stitch.

16 With the block on the pressing surface, fold back the top half and press it against the seam allowances.

17 The block will measure 12½ inches square. Make an additional 17 blocks, for a total of 18 blocks.

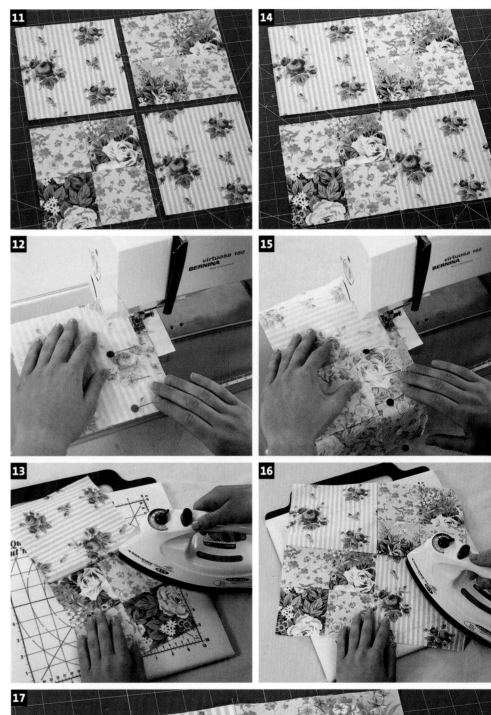

Assembling the Duvet Cover

18 If your chenille is striped, like the chenille shown here, look at it carefully and measure to determine the best place to make cuts. Using the 12-inch-square ruler, scissors, and a fabric marker, measure, mark, and cut 17 chenille squares, each 12½ by 12½ inches.

19 Lay out the patchwork blocks and chenille squares as shown below, making sure the blocks are oriented in the same direction. Pin and stitch the blocks and squares to make rows. Press the seam allowances away from the chenille squares. Join the rows, butting the seam allowances. Press the seam allowances in one direction to complete the cover top.

Adding the Edging

20 From the edging fabric, measure, mark, and cut 2-inch-wide crosswise strips (from selvage to selvage) to total the perimeter of the cover top, plus several inches for joining seams. Join the strips to make one long strip. From this strip cut two strips the exact width of the cover top and two strips the exact length of the cover top. Fold each strip in half lengthwise with wrong sides together and press.

21 Open a strip on one end and turn under ¼ inch; finger-press, then refold the strip. Right sides together and raw edges aligned, pin the folded strip to a corresponding edge on the cover top (a longer strip to a side edge, a shorter strip to the top or bottom), starting a little more than ¼ inch from a corner. When you approach the other end, trim the strip even with the edge of the cover top. Open the strip and turn under the end a little more than ¼ inch. Finish pinning the strip to the edge. Baste the strip to the edge.

22 Repeat to join another strip to an adjoining edge. You should have a small square, slightly larger than ¼ inch, of the cover top showing at the corner. Repeat to join strips to the remaining edges.

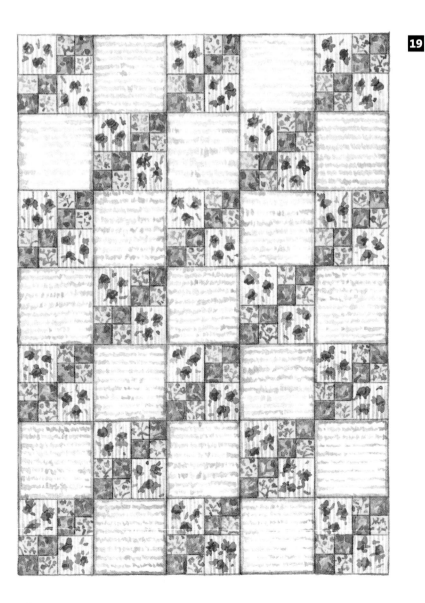

19

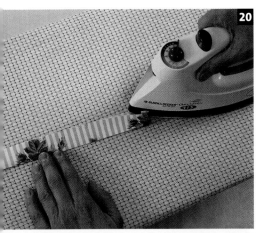

Backing the Cover Top

23 Cut the sheet for the backing the same width as and 12 inches longer than the cover top. This extra length will enable you to make an envelope closure.

24 Measure and mark a crosswise line 18 inches from one end of the backing. Cut along this line. On each piece, turn under ½ inch of the raw edge you just cut and press. Turn the raw edge in to meet the fold and press again; pin. Hem each edge by machine. On the short piece, make five equally spaced buttonholes across the width, ½ inch from the hemmed edge.

25 Lay out the backing pieces right side up, lapping the short piece over the long piece so that together they equal the length of the cover top. Mark the button positions through the buttonholes; stitch the buttons to the long piece.

26 Button the backing. Lay the cover top, right side down, on the backing; pin and stitch all the way around. Unbutton the backing and turn the cover right side out. Gently pull outward on the edging and finger-press. Slip a duvet into the cover and button closed.

1 yard of lace fabric or
lace curtain panel

Fabric scissors

Repositionable spray
adhesive

Latex paint to match
your wall

White latex paint

Disposable
paint sprayer,
available at paint
stores

DO IT TODAY

Lacy Stenciled Walls

TRADITIONAL STENCILS TYPICALLY CREATE crisp edges and bold shapes, but
you can achieve a softer look using a piece of lace. Choose a pattern that con-
tains distinct, fairly isolated designs. You can use lace fabric from a fabric
store or look for ready-made lace curtain panels in the linen section of a
department store. Before you start to stencil your walls, practice on a piece of
plywood or hardboard painted your wall color.

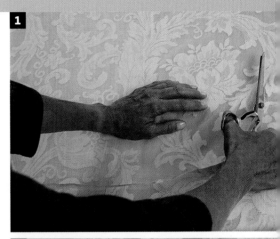

1 Look carefully at your lace to determine which part of the design you want to transfer to the wall. Cut out that area, including a generous perimeter of fabric around it.

2 Working outdoors, spray the wrong side of the lace with repositionable adhesive. If you're using lace fabric, the wrong side looks less finished than the right side. The wrong side of a lace curtain panel is the hemmed side.

3 Position the lace on the wall and smooth it over the surface, applying just enough pressure to make it stick.

4 Mix your wall paint with white paint to create a lighter, almost white, version of your wall color. Follow the paint-sprayer manufacturer's instructions for adding the paint. Holding the sprayer upright and working back and forth evenly, apply a fine coat of paint over the lace.

5 Allow the paint to dry at least 5 minutes. Gently peel off the lace to reveal the design. Repeat at other places on the walls, varying the spacing and height to create a random pattern.

TIP

IF YOU WANT MIRROR-IMAGE DESIGNS TO APPEAR ON YOUR WALL, YOU'LL NEED TO CUT TWO STENCILS, ONE WITH THE PATTERN FACING ONE DIRECTION, THE OTHER WITH THE PATTERN FACING THE OPPOSITE DIRECTION. IF THE LACE DOESN'T HAVE MIRROR IMAGES, CUT TWO PIECES OF THE SAME DESIGN AND TURN ONE OVER WHEN YOU STENCIL.

Fine Linen Specialists

Miller's Cleaners & Dyers

We're Dyeing to Serve You!

Wood Hanger Window Treatment

A LARGER-THAN-LIFE REPLICA of a vintage coat hanger makes a fanciful top treatment for a single window. The hanger and stationary tulle panels are easy to create using materials available at a home center and a fabric store. A blueprint service can enlarge a photocopy of a real hanger to serve as a pattern. You'll need adequate space above the window to accommodate an oversize hook.

TIP

FLEA MARKETS ARE GOOD SOURCES FOR A WOOD COAT HANGER THAT YOU CAN USE FOR A PATTERN. LOOK FOR ONE WITH A GRACEFUL SHAPE AND UPTURNED ENDS.

MATERIALS

Wood coat hanger

Tracing paper

¾-inch plywood

Eye and ear protection

Jigsaw

Palm sander

White or off-white latex paint

Clean rag

Graphite paper

Acrylic craft paint

Small paintbrush

Nails

Fence stay, long enough for hook plus several inches, available at home centers

Wire snips

Poultry nails

Fabric scissors

White tulle, 118 inches wide and the length of the window frame plus 15 inches

White thread

10 yards of white satin ribbon, ⅜ inch wide

Two rubber bands

Two pushpins

Hook or other hanging device for wall

Making the Pattern

1 Measure the width of your window, including the window frame, then add 6 inches. The extra width will allow the tulle panels to clear the frame.

2 Copy your wood coat hanger at a photocopy shop. Take the photocopy to a blueprint service and ask for an enlargement to the width determined in Step 1.

Making the Coat Hanger

3 Trace the enlarged hanger, minus the hook, onto sheets of tracing paper taped together. It's easiest to trace with the pattern taped to a window or sliding door. Cut out the pattern.

4 Lay the pattern on the plywood and draw around the edges with a pencil. Wearing eye and ear protection, cut out the hanger with a jigsaw.

5 Using a palm sander, sand the hanger's edges to make them look slightly worn.

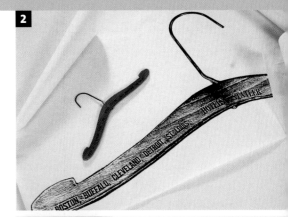

6 Dilute the latex paint to the consistency of half-and-half. Using a rag, wipe the paint mixture onto the front of the hanger.

7 Using a computer and printer, create and print the wording for your hanger; enlarge it at a photocopy shop. Trace the wording onto the paper pattern, following the curve of the hanger.

8 Position graphite paper, graphite side down, on the hanger. Place the pattern on top. Using a pencil, out-line the letters with moderate pressure, transferring them to the wood.

9 With acrylic craft paint and a paintbrush, fill in the letters.

10 Refer to the curve of the hook on your original hanger to shape the fence stay by hand. Or, draw an enlarged version on a scrap of plywood and cut out the piece to make a form for shaping the fence stay. Nail the form through the paper pattern to your work surface, then place two more nails below

the form and one nail to the right. Wrap the stay around the form and nails as shown. Use wire snips to cut off any excess length.

11 Attach the shaped fence-stay hook to the back of the hanger with poultry nails.

Making the Tulle Curtains

12 Cut the tulle in half length-wise to create two panels. Make narrow, single-fold hems by machine on the lengthwise edges.

13 At the unfinished edges (at top and bottom), lap the ribbon over the front of the tulle and stitch by machine, turning under the rib-bon ends at the start and finish.

14 Cut the remaining ribbon in half. Gather up each tulle panel approximately 5 inches from one end and secure with a rubber band. Tie a length of ribbon around each panel at the rubber band.

Installing the Treatment

15 On the back of the hanger, insert a pushpin at each end. Hook the rubber bands over the pushpins.

16 Ask two helpers to hold the hanger above the window so it clears the frame by a few inches. Mark the hanger position on the wall, install the hook, and mount the treatment.

SEWING WORKSHOP

Slipcovered Lamp Shade

SLIPCOVERING A LAMP SHADE is a quick and easy way to reinvent a lamp. This "slip," as slipcovers are called in the design world, matches the duvet cover, but it would be just as charming in fabrics with a similar cottage floral look. (Choose fabrics with a pale background to allow maximum light to come through the shade.) A plate with gently scalloped edges is the perfect template for the skirt pattern.

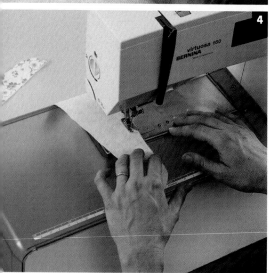

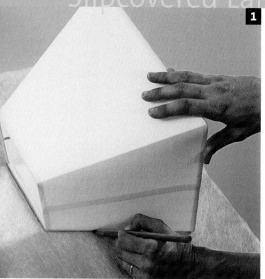

Cutting the Pieces

1 Lay one side of the lamp shade on the pattern material or interfacing and trace the shape. Add a ¼-inch seam allowance to each edge. Cut out the pattern piece.

2 Lay a scalloped plate facedown on the pattern material or interfacing and trace as much of the shape as desired for the bottom of the skirt. (The finished skirt should be about ¼ inch narrower on each end than the shade's side; see the photo in Step 8.) Draw a straight line for the top of the skirt. Add a ¼-inch seam allowance to each edge. Cut out the pattern piece.

3 Using the patterns, cut four side pieces, four side lining pieces, four skirt pieces, and four skirt lining pieces from the fabrics.

Making the Slipcover

4 Right sides together and raw edges aligned, sew a skirt lining piece to a skirt piece using a ¼-inch seam allowance, leaving the straight edge open. Trim the seam allowances to ⅛ inch; turn and press. Repeat to join the remaining skirt and skirt lining pieces.

TIP

A CHARMING ALTERNATIVE TO A SCALLOPED SKIRT IS ONE THAT'S STRAIGHT ON THE BOTTOM, ESPECIALLY IF THE SKIRT FABRIC IS STRIPED. KEEP THE SKIRT LENGTH IN PROPORTION TO THE SCALE OF THE SHADE. ON A SMALL SHADE SUCH AS THIS ONE, 1½ INCHES IS A GOOD FINISHED LENGTH. (DON'T FORGET TO ADD SEAM ALLOWANCES.)

5

8 Turn the side piece right side out. Turn under the lining ¼ inch at the opening and slipstitch closed; press. Repeat with the remaining side and skirt pieces.

9 With wrong sides together, pin two sections along one edge.

10 Stitch the sections with a narrow seam allowance, creating a finished seam on the outside. Repeat with the other sections to complete the slipcover. Sew a button at each corner on each section. Slip over the lamp shade.

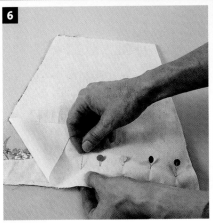

6

7

8

9

5 Right sides together and raw edges aligned, baste a skirt section made in Step 4 to the bottom edge of a side piece.

6 Lay a side lining piece on top, as shown. Pin.

7 Stitch around the edges using a ¼-inch seam allowance, backstitching at the beginning and end and leaving a 3-inch opening along the bottom edge for turning. Trim the corners to reduce bulk.

27

Hand-me-down Treasures

Doll Quilt

ABOVE: What little girl wouldn't love to have a doll quilt to match her duvet cover? This one, made of half-scale blocks and chenille squares, even sports the same edging— only half as wide, of course.

Heirloom Dress

LEFT: **This hand-sewn dress, another family heirloom, is displayed as a work of art on an antique hook painted white.**

Whitewashed Table

BELOW LEFT: **An unfinished pedestal table passed down through four generations became a harmonious part of the scheme. It was first whitewashed with a dilute mixture of white latex paint and water, then scrubbed with fine steel wool to reveal its lovely grain and delicate detailing.**

Patchwork Chair Cushion

BELOW: **Wide-wale chenille left over from the duvet cover trims a cushion made from a vintage patchwork pillow sham found at a flea market.**

Shared Space

TWO SISTERS SHARE THIS high-ceilinged bedroom featuring a dramatic arched window. Peach paint warms the walls; crisp pleated curtains and bas-relief designs frame the window and draw attention to the sweeping view of distant hills. Placing the bunk bed on the diagonal frees up wall space and breaks up the room in an interesting way, while "slipcovers" stitched from a quilt, bedspreads made from cotton-duck shower curtains, and puffy bolsters created from a curtain panel soften the look of the metal bed frame. Simple shelves provide a place to display the girls' treasures. All in all, it's a room that says "ours."

A south-facing arched window begged for a window treatment that was both decorative and hardworking; bunk beds conserved floor space but took up the only uninterrupted wall in the room.

Bas-relief Walls

BAS-RELIEF—from the French words for "low" and "raised work"—is a technique for creating sculptural decoration that stands out slightly from the wall. Here it accentuates the dramatic curve of the arched window, but you can use this technique for a rectangular window as well (see page 35). The dimensional quality comes from applying joint compound, tinted with your paint color, through a stencil and onto the wall. This long design calls for two stencils, the second one a continuation of the first. Positioning is key when you're working with more than one stencil; read Steps 5 and 6 before you begin.

TIP

WASH AND DRY THE STEN-

CILS THOROUGHLY AFTER

EACH APPLICATION. YOU

MUST REMOVE ALL THE

JOINT COMPOUND BECAUSE

YOU WILL FLIP THE STENCILS

TO MAKE A MIRROR-IMAGE

DESIGN ON THE OTHER

SIDE OF THE WINDOW.

MATERIALS

Purchased
plastic stencil

Stencil plastic*

Masking tape*

Fine-point permanent
marker*

Rotary cutting mat,
available at fabric
stores and quilt shops*

Craft knife*

Repositionable spray
adhesive

Blue painter's tape

Latex paint the color
of the walls

Water-based joint
compound

Plastic drop cloth

Palette knife

Iridescent glitter powder
and stencil brush
(optional)

*Required only
if you're enlarging a
purchased stencil.*

Step by Step

Cutting the Stencils

1 If you find a stencil that's just the right design and size, skip to Step 3. If you purchase a stencil that's not large enough, trace the design onto paper and enlarge it, in sections if necessary, on a photo-copy machine. To make the sections align properly, draw the beginning motif from the second section onto the end of the first one; this shape will be a "reference motif."

2 Lay the stencil plastic over the design; anchor the stencil with masking tape. Mark the outlines, including those of the reference motif, with the permanent marker. Mark an X on the reference motif.

With the cutting mat underneath, carefully cut out all the shapes except the reference motif using the craft knife.

Stenciling the Design

3 Measure carefully and lightly mark the design's position on the wall. Spray the back of the first (or only) stencil with the adhesive; press the stencil to the wall and anchor the edges with painter's tape.

4 Mix a small amount of your wall paint with the joint compound. Make sure the compound mixture is significantly lighter than the walls, with just a whisper of color, or the bas-relief won't be visible.

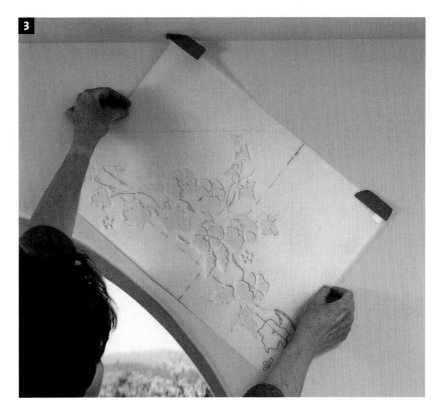

5 Cover your work area with a drop cloth. Using the palette knife, apply the compound mixture over the stencil. Don't scrape the knife flat against the stencil, but instead try for a raised, slightly dimensional effect. Note the outlined (but not cut out) leaf with the X marked inside; this shape is the reference motif for the placement of the continuing stencil.

6 If you have a two-part design, position the continuing stencil on top of the first one while the compound mixture is still wet, lining up the reference motif. Here the cutout leaf shape on the continuing stencil is positioned over the X-marked leaf shape on the first stencil. Tape the continuing stencil to the wall at the outer edge of the design.

7 Holding the continuing stencil in place with one hand, carefully remove the first stencil. (Use a helper if you need to.) Anchor the remaining edges of the continuing stencil with painter's tape and apply the joint compound.

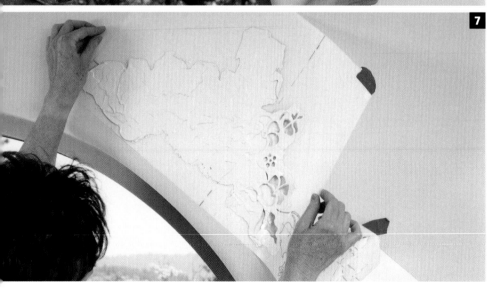

8 Carefully remove the stencil. Wash and dry all the stencils. Flip them to stencil the area on the opposite side of the window.

9 Allow the joint compound to dry. You can leave the relief areas plain, as shown here, or brush them with iridescent glitter powder.

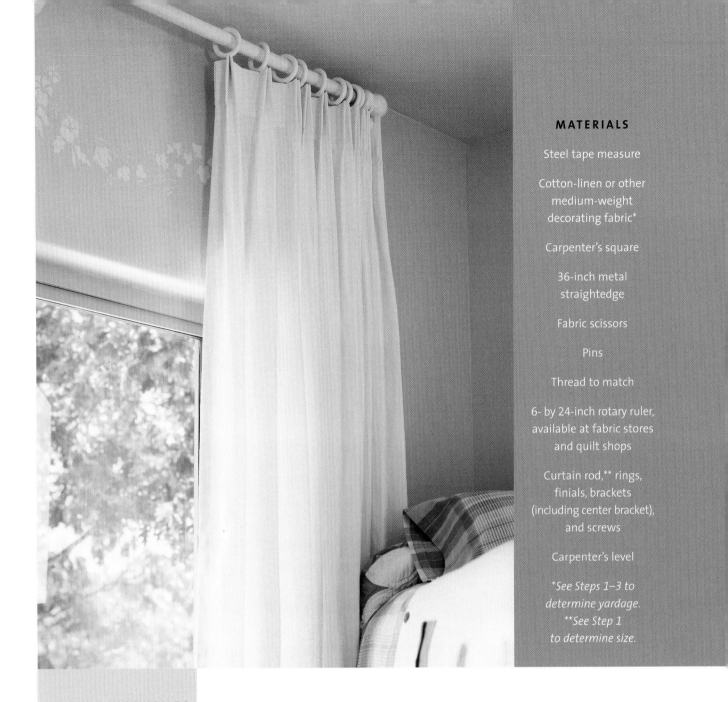

MATERIALS

Steel tape measure

Cotton-linen or other medium-weight decorating fabric*

Carpenter's square

36-inch metal straightedge

Fabric scissors

Pins

Thread to match

6- by 24-inch rotary ruler, available at fabric stores and quilt shops

Curtain rod,** rings, finials, brackets (including center bracket), and screws

Carpenter's level

*See Steps 1–3 to determine yardage.
**See Step 1 to determine size.

SEWING WORKSHOP

Paris-pleat Curtains

PLEATED CURTAINS FRAME the room's windows and keep out late-afternoon glare. This variation on the classic French, or pinch, pleat has two rather than the traditional three folds in each pleat, and the folds are tacked at the top rather than at the base, creating a slight fanned effect. The simple-to-sew treatment features unlined panels that open and close by hand.

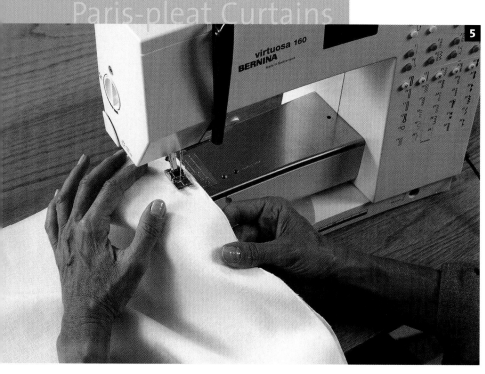

Calculating Yardage

1 To determine the finished width of the window treatment, measure your window's width, including the frame, if any. For curtain panels that open to expose the entire glass area, you'll need to allow for "stackback" (room on either side of the window to push the curtain panels off the glass): measure the width of the glass, then add one-third of that number to arrive at the finished width. The finished width is also the rod size.

2 Multiply the finished width by 2 for pleat fullness. Add 12 inches to allow for side hems. Divide the total by the width of the fabric (typically 54 inches for home decorating fabrics) to arrive at the number of fabric widths needed, rounding any fraction up or down to the nearest whole number. Exception: If the number of widths is 1 plus *any* fraction, you must round *up* to 2.

3 Decide approximately how far above the window you want the treatment to be mounted. From that point, measure to the floor for curtain length. Add 8 inches for the heading and 8 inches for the hem. This is the cut length. Multiply that number by the widths needed, determined in Step 2, and divide by 36 inches for the yards needed; add 1 yard for good measure. This number is the total yardage needed.

Cutting and Joining the Pieces

4 Carefully square off one cut end across the width of your fabric using a carpenter's square and a metal straightedge. From the squared-off end, measure down each selvage edge of the fabric the distance equal to the cut length (see Step 3); clip the selvages at this point. Mark and cut across the fabric (do not tear) between the clips. Repeat to cut the required number of pieces (see Step 2). Carefully trim off the selvages on each piece.

5 Right sides together and raw edges aligned, join half the pieces to form each panel, using a ½-inch seam allowance. If you have an odd number of pieces, cut one piece in half vertically and stitch each half to a whole panel. Finish the raw edges on the seams and press the seam allowances open. You will now have two flat curtain panels, one for each side of the window.

Stitching the Hems

6 On the vertical edges of each curtain panel, turn in 3 inches, wrong sides together, and press. Unfold and turn each raw edge in to meet the fold; pin. Stitch close to the fold to form the hem.

7 At the upper (heading) and lower (hem) edges of each panel, turn in 8 inches, wrong sides together, and press. Unfold and turn the raw edge in to meet the fold; pin. Stitch close to the fold.

Making the Pleats

8 To determine the number of pleats per panel, multiply the number of full fabric widths in each panel by 5, and the half-widths by 2. Add the numbers together. (The number of spaces between pleats will be 1 less than the number of pleats; note this number for use in Step 10.)

9 To arrive at the pleat size, or fabric allowance for each pleat, subtract half the finished width of the entire treatment, determined in Step 1, from the width of each

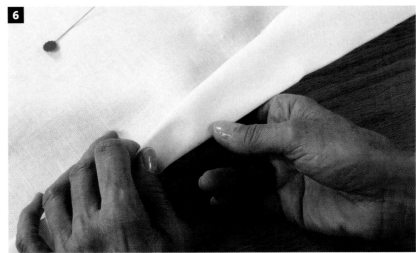

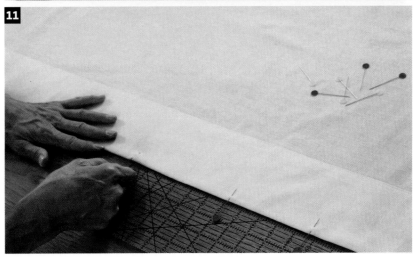

seamed panel and divide by the number of pleats, determined in Step 8. Round off to the nearest ¼ inch.

10 To determine the space between pleats, first subtract 3 inches from the finished width of each panel. (You will want to begin a pleat just inside the side hem stitching, not at the outer edge.) Divide that number by the number of spaces between pleats, determined in Step 8, to arrive at the fabric allowance for each space. Round off to the nearest ¼ inch.

11 Lay one of the flat panels on your work surface, wrong side up. Place the first pin just inside the side hem stitching to mark the start of the first pleat. Measure and pin the end of the first pleat (from Step 9); then measure and pin the first space (from Step 10). Continue across the panel, alternating pleats and spaces. Ideally, your last pleat will end at the side hem stitching; in reality, you'll probably need to adjust some pleats. Make adjustments in the pleats only, not in the spaces. Repeat to pin the second panel.

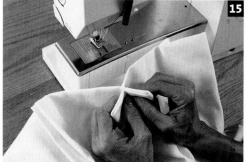

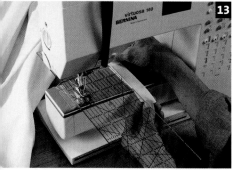

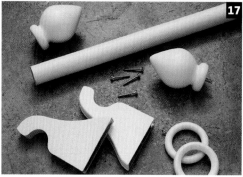

15 Working with one pleat at a time, push down on the pleat loop, flattening it against the pleat stitching and dividing it equally into two smaller loops. Bring the folds together to make a two-fold pleat; pin at the folds. Continue making pleats across both panels.

16 Holding the pleat securely and working at the very top of the heading, stitch forward and backward several times through all layers, keeping the stitches short, to bar-tack the pleat. Repeat to bar-tack all the pleats.

Installing the Treatment

17 Gather the curtain rod, rings, finials, brackets, and screws. Sew the rings to the pleats at the pleat stitching (not at the bar tacks).

18 Thread the treatment onto the rod and place it in the end brackets. Have two helpers hold the treatment up, centered precisely on the window, so that the panels hang ¼ to ½ inch from the floor covering. (Do not measure down from the ceiling line; it may not be straight.) Mark the wall lightly at the top of each bracket.

19 Follow the manufacturer's instructions to install the brackets, using a carpenter's level to make sure the rod is straight.

12 Starting at one edge, on the wrong side, bring the first two pins together so a pleat "loop" is created on the right side; pin the pleat as shown. Continue pinning pleats across the width of the panel, ending with a pleat at the side hem stitching. Repeat to pin pleats for the second panel.

Stitching the Pleats

13 To create a seam guide for stitching the pleats, divide the pleat size by 2. Lay your rotary ruler under the sewing machine needle at this measurement. Layer several strips of masking tape and place the stacked strips on the faceplate along the right-hand edge of the ruler. Remove the ruler.

14 On the right side of the fabric, stitch each pleat loop from the top of the heading to the lower edge of the heading, using the seam guide as shown. Backstitch at the lower edge of the heading.

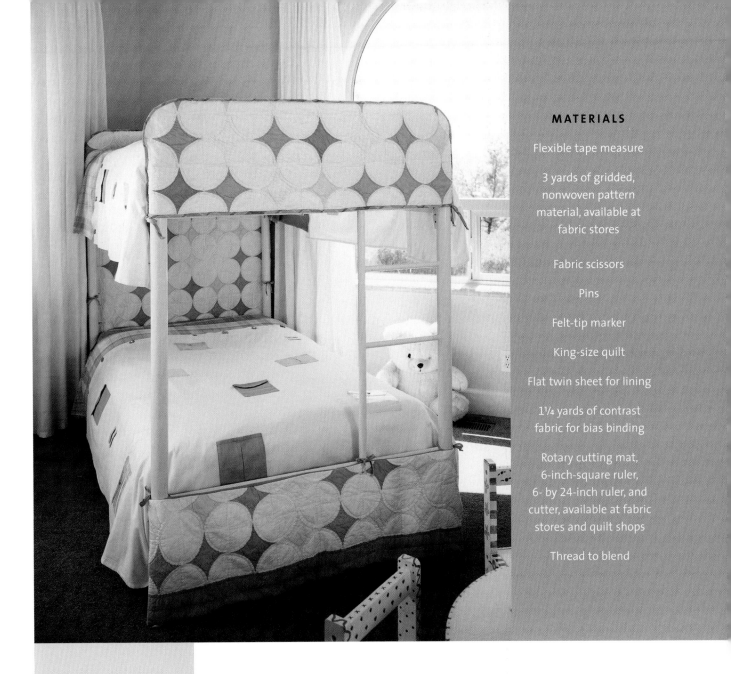

MATERIALS

Flexible tape measure

3 yards of gridded,
nonwoven pattern
material, available at
fabric stores

Fabric scissors

Pins

Felt-tip marker

King-size quilt

Flat twin sheet for lining

1¼ yards of contrast
fabric for bias binding

Rotary cutting mat,
6-inch-square ruler,
6- by 24-inch ruler, and
cutter, available at fabric
stores and quilt shops

Thread to blend

SEWING WORKSHOP

Slipcovered Bed

INEXPENSIVE QUILTS found at bed-and-bath stores and through home cata-
logs make great "fabric" for soft furnishings. Here, a king-size quilt became
bunk-bed slipcovers, adding lively color, pattern, and texture to the room's
scheme. Be sure to prewash your quilt in cold water with a mild, nonbleach
detergent; dry on medium heat. Then, measure the quilt and make a cutting
layout as described in the steps that follow.

Making the Patterns

1 Measure the height and width of the top bunk's footboard. Cut two pieces of pattern material, each several inches larger than these measurements on all edges. Loosely pin the pieces together on the top and sides.

2 Slip the pattern material "envelope" over the footboard. Working outward from the top center, repin the top and sides, striving for a smooth fit around any curves. Mark the position of the bottom crosspiece with pins across the width of the frame. Remove the envelope from the footboard.

3 Using a felt-tip marker, draw over the pins on all edges to create stitching lines, then add and mark your seam allowance (see the tip at left). Remove the pins and cut out one pattern piece.

4 You'll use this pattern in Step 6 to cut out two pieces for the footboard and one piece for the headboard. You'll also use it to cut out the long headboard piece. For the length of this piece, measure from the top of the frame to the floor; add your seam allowance to the bottom.

5 For the skirt at the foot of the bottom bunk, measure the height and width of the lower frame. Make a pattern, adding seam allowances to all edges.

6 To ensure that you can cut all the needed pieces from your quilt and lining, make quick sketches of both and note their dimensions. Measure your pattern pieces and draw rough cutting layouts on your sketches. Then, using your patterns, cut out the following pieces from the quilt: three footboard pieces,

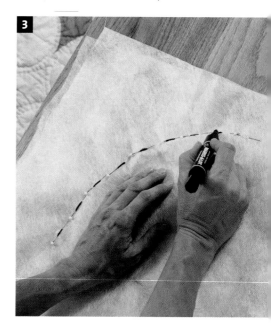

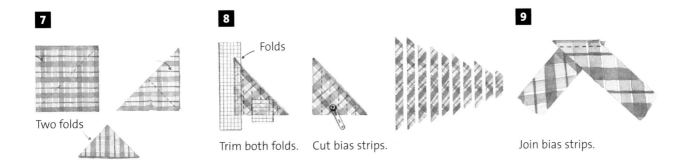

7

8 Folds

Trim both folds. Cut bias strips.

9 Join bias strips.

one long headboard piece, and one piece for the skirt. From the lining cut one long headboard piece and one piece for the skirt.

Making the Bias Binding

7 Bias binding trims the head-board and footboard slipcovers and forms the ties. To make the bias strips, cut the binding fabric into a 42-inch square. Fold the square in half diagonally and press. Fold the piece diagonally again and press.

8 Place the folded piece on your cutting mat. Align the square ruler precisely with the lower folded edge, as shown. Place the long ruler just over the double folds, butting it against the square ruler. Remove the square ruler. Using your rotary cutter, make a clean cut to remove the double folds, then cut 2½-inch-wide strips.

9 Using a ¼-inch seam allowance, join the strips as shown to make one long strip. Press the seams open. Fold the strip in half lengthwise, wrong sides together, and press.

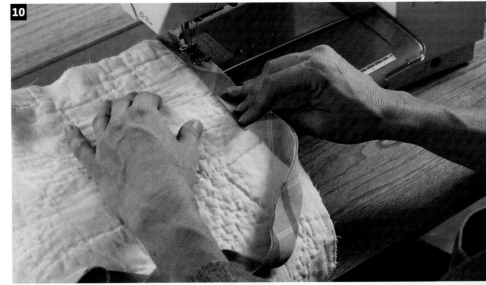

10

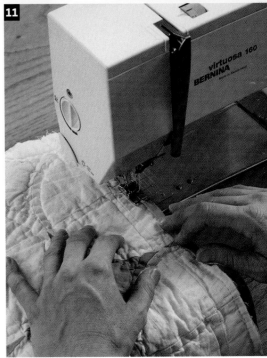

11

Sewing the Slipcovers

10 Start with the slipcover pieces for the foot of the top bunk. Working on the wrong side of one piece, align the raw edges of the bias binding with the piece's bottom edge; stitch, using your seam allowance. Cut off the excess binding strip.

11 Turn the quilt piece right side up. Bring the binding to the front, covering the previous stitching with the binding's folded edge. Topstitch close to the fold through all thick-nesses. Repeat to bind the bottom edge of the second piece.

12

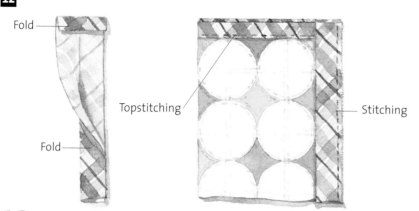

Fold

Topstitching

Fold

Stitching

12 Place the two pieces wrong sides together. To join and bind the edges in one step, open up one end of the remaining binding strip, turn the end in approximately ¼ inch, and finger-press; refold the strip lengthwise. Starting at the lower edges, pin the raw edges of the binding to the pieces, easing in the fullness around any curves. Stitch the binding to the pieces.

13 When you get to within approximately 3 inches of the opposite end, cut the strip approximately ¼ inch beyond the edges; open and turn in the end of the strip, refold it, and finish stitching the seam.

14 As you did on the bottom edges, bring the binding to the front and topstitch close to the fold.

15 To make the ties, turn the raw edges of the remaining binding strip in to meet the fold; refold, pin, and stitch. Cut seven ties to twice the desired length and knot each end. Fold in half to make double ties. Hand-sew one tie to each bottom corner of the footboard slipcover you just made. (You'll later sew two ties

to the headboard slipcover and three to the skirt.)

16 Measure the completed footboard slipcover from the top center of the upper binding to the bottom center of the lower-edge binding. Note this measurement for the next step.

17 To make the headboard slipcover, place the long quilt piece and the long lining piece with right sides together and raw edges aligned. From the center of the top edge, measure to the length determined in Step 16. Mark this point on each side by making a clip, through both layers, equal to the width of your seam allowance.

18 Pin the pieces together from the clips down and across the bottom; stitch. Trim the lower corners to reduce bulk. Turn the slipcover right side out and press the stitched edges.

13

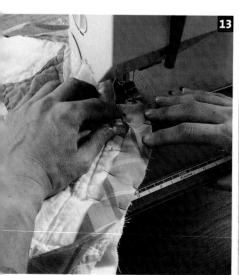

14

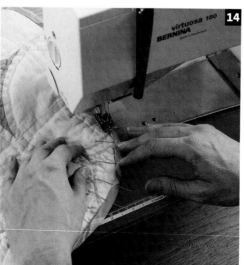

17

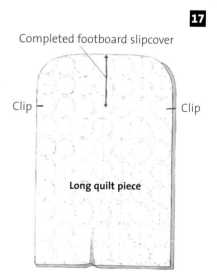

Completed footboard slipcover

Clip

Clip

Long quilt piece

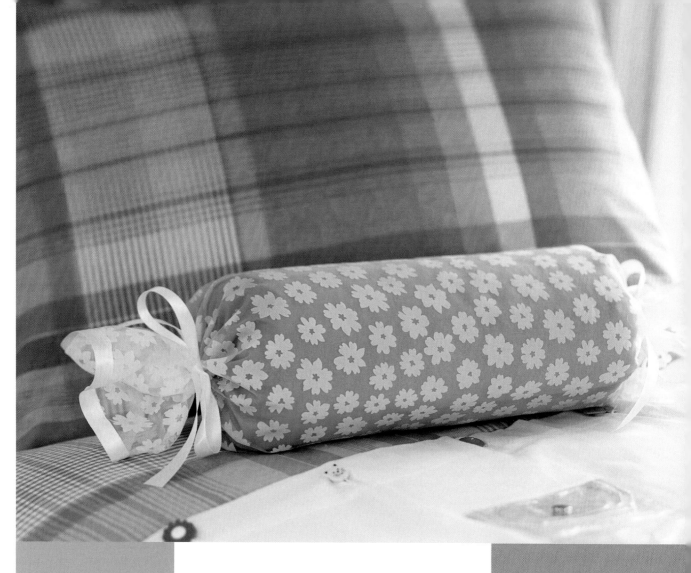

Sheer-covered Bolster

THIS QUICK-AND-EASY BOLSTER is the perfect little pillow for girls who love ribbon and lace. The bolster form consists of a piece of batting that's been rolled up and glued together; a solid-color inner cover cinches up neatly at the ends. The outer cover was made from a semisheer curtain panel; satin ribbon keeps the bolster form in place and trims the edges.

FINISHED SIZE 14 inches long, not including the gathered ends

MATERIALS

Fabric scissors

½ yard of high-loft polyester quilt batting, 48 inches wide

Hot-glue gun

⅝ yard of solid-color fabric

Thread to match or blend

1½ yards of satin ribbon, ¼ inch wide

⅝ yard of semisheer fabric or curtain panel

Spray starch or spray sizing

2½ yards of double-faced satin ribbon, ⅝ inch wide

44

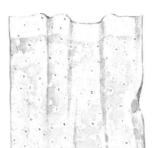

TIP

PATTERNED SHEER AND

SEMISHEER FABRICS ARE

WIDELY AVAILABLE BY THE YARD

AT FABRIC STORES, ESPECIALLY

THOSE SPECIALIZING IN HOME

DECORATING FABRICS. MOST

SHEERS ARE WHITE OR ECRU.

THEY ARE TYPICALLY 54 INCHES

WIDE—SOME ARE AS WIDE AS

118 INCHES—WHICH WILL

ALLOW YOU TO MAKE SEVERAL

BOLSTERS FROM MINIMAL

YARDAGE.

Making the Bolster and Inner Cover

1 Cut the batting 14 inches long, across the width of the piece. Roll the batting into a 14-inch-long "sausage" and glue the edge using the glue gun. The thickness of the form will vary depending on the loft of the batting piece.

2 From the solid-color fabric, measure, mark, and cut a piece to cover the bolster. The width should equal the measurement around the form plus 1 inch for seam allowances; the length should be 14 inches plus the measurement across one end of the form plus 1 inch for the ribbon casings.

3 On the edges that will cover the ends of the form, turn under ½ inch to the wrong side of the fabric and press to make a ribbon casing.

4 Open out the casings. With right sides together and the unpressed edges aligned, pin and stitch the piece, using a ½-inch seam allowance, to form a tube.

5 Press the seam allowances open. Refold and re-press the casings. At one end, lay a length of ¼-inch satin ribbon inside the casing, leaving a few inches of ribbon free. Stitch the casing ⅛ inch from the raw edge, being careful not to catch the ribbon in

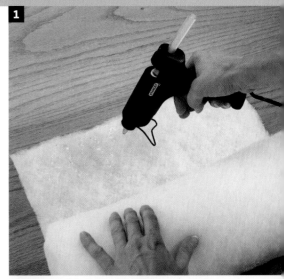

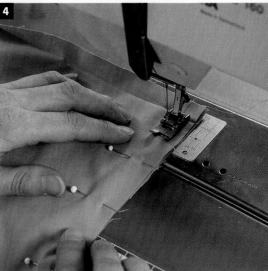

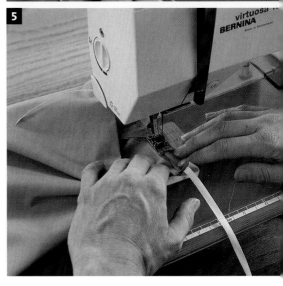

the stitching. Leave a 1-inch opening on the casing to cinch up the ribbon. Repeat on the other end. Turn the bolster cover right side out.

6 Insert the form into the cover, pulling it through to center it. Pull each ribbon tight and tie it into a bow. Tuck the ribbon ends inside the cover.

Making the Outer Cover

7 From the semisheer fabric, cut a piece the length of the bolster (14 inches) plus 16 inches by the measurement around the bolster plus 1 inch for seam allowances. Spray the fabric with spray starch or spray sizing, following the instructions on the can.

8 Lay the fabric right side up. On the edges that will be trimmed with ribbon, turn up 1/4 inch and

press; then turn up another 1/4 inch and press. Lap a piece of 5/8-inch double-faced satin ribbon over each turned-up edge. Stitch close to the inner edge of the ribbon, hemming the edge and attaching the ribbon at the same time. Repeat to stitch ribbon to the other end. This side will be the right side of the cover.

9 Right sides together and raw edges aligned, pin and stitch the remaining edges of the piece using a 1/2-inch seam allowance. Turn the cover right side out.

10 Slip the bolster into the semisheer cover and center it. Cut the remaining 5/8-inch ribbon into two pieces; tie them into bows around the semisheer fabric as close as possible to the ends of the bolster and fluff the ribbon-trimmed edges.

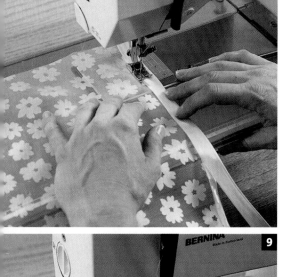

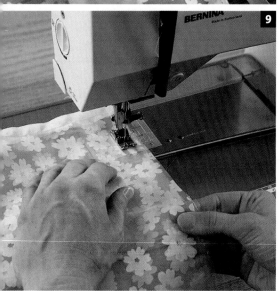

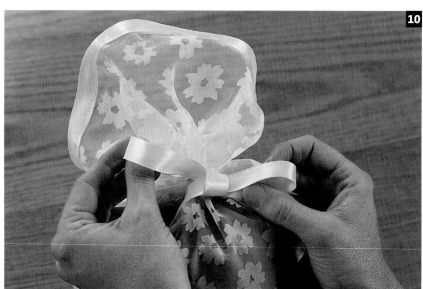

Miter box and backsaw
or a chop saw

Wiggle molding, four
times the desired length
of the shelves, plus 2
feet for the end pieces
(for two shelves)

2-by-2 lumber, twice the
desired length of the
shelves, plus 6 inches
for miscuts (for two
shelves)

Electric brad nailer
and 20-gauge nails, or
tack hammer and small
finishing nails

Wood glue

Wood filler or
all-purpose spackling
compound

100-grit sandpaper

Latex primer and paint

Small hammer

18-gauge brass pins,
available at home centers
and hardware stores

24-gauge wire
for beading

Glass or plastic beads
(or a combination)

Wire snips

Long-nose
(needle-nose) pliers

Self-leveling picture-
frame hangers with a
saw-toothed edge

IN A WEEKEND

Wiggle Shelves

"WIGGLE MOLDING" is, in fact, the real name for the curvy wood molding used to support corrugated metal roofing. Here it does a fine job as painted and beaded shelves that hold the girls' artwork and family photos. The molding is inexpensive and readily available in various lengths at home centers. Examine the molding carefully when you shop; the occasional piece is warped.

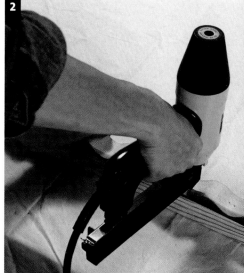

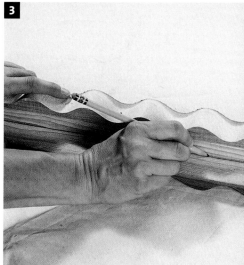

A WORD TO THE NOVICE: YOU
MAY NOTICE THAT A PIECE OF
LUMBER IDENTIFIED AS A 2 BY
2 ACTUALLY MEASURES 1½ BY
1½ INCHES. THE DIMENSION
IT'S SOLD BY IS THE CUT SIZE;
THE WOOD SHRINKS AS IT
DRIES. YOU DON'T NEED TO
MAKE ANY ADJUSTMENTS TO
THIS PROJECT BECAUSE OF
THIS DIFFERENCE.

Assembling and Painting the Shelves

1 Using a miter box and backsaw or a chop saw, cut four pieces of wiggle molding the desired length of the shelves, cutting each piece in a "valley" rather than on a "hill." Set the remaining length of molding aside for the end caps. Cut two pieces of the 2 by 2 the same length as the wiggle molding. *The following instructions are for one shelf; repeat for a second shelf.*

2 Place the molding on top of the 2 by 2 and nail the pieces together in the valleys as shown. (When turned right side up later, this unit will be the support for the art and photos.)

3 With the support unit still oriented the same way, set another piece of molding, with its wiggles down, against the unit; draw a line on the unit along the edge of the molding.

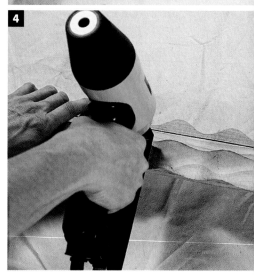

4 Lay the marked piece on its side as shown. Flip the free piece of molding so the wiggles face up and the edge aligns with the pencil line. (This piece of molding will form the ledge of the shelf.) Nail the molding to the 2 by 2, placing the nails in the valleys. Be sure the hills line up on the two molding pieces.

5 From the leftover molding, mark two end caps equal in length to the depth of the shelf, making the marks in the valley as shown.

6 Cut the pieces. You may need to trim them a bit to fit.

7 Glue a cap piece at each end of the shelf so it aligns with the ledge.

8 Fill the cracks and nail holes with wood filler or all-purpose spackling compound. When it's dry, sand the shelves, then prime and paint them.

Beading and Mounting the Shelves

9 Hammer a brass pin about ¼ inch deep into each hill of the ledge, zigzagging the position of the pins as shown.

10 Wind the 24-gauge wire around the first pin several times, leaving the wire end free. String beads onto the wire and loop the wire over the second pin. Continue stringing beads and looping the wire from pin to pin. At the end of the shelf, wind the wire around the last pin. Trim the wire at the start and finish and tuck under the ends with long-nose pliers.

11 Mount the shelf on the wall using the self-leveling picture-frame hangers.

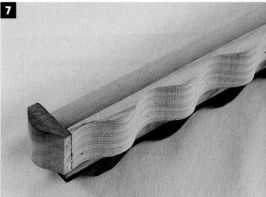

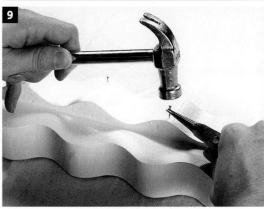

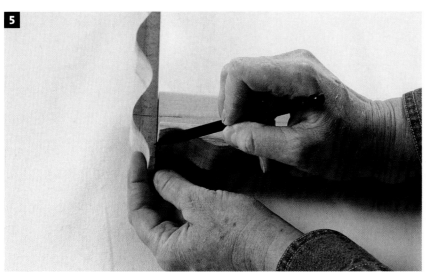

Denim Days

A LITTLE PAINT AND FABRIC turned an upstairs room with a window wall and sloping ceilings into a bonus room for daytime play. Denim is the common denominator here: the painted wall mimics the look of this kid-friendly fabric, while real denim in the duvet cover, boxed floor cushions, pillow shams, and purchased beanbag chair stands up to heavy use. Bright painted squares on the floor reiterate the intense colors in the bedding and the accessories. Wall cupboards and simple storage cubes provide plenty of places to stow "stuff." It's no wonder everyone wants to come over to play.

An attic room with a view was not much more than a catchall space; white walls and a plywood floor begged for reinvention.

MATERIALS

Rotary cutter, cutting mat, and 6- by 24-inch rotary ruler, available at fabric stores and quilt shops

$1/8$ yard *each* of 12 fabrics for Round 1*

$1/8$ yard *each* of 12 fabrics for Round 2*

$1/4$ yard *each* of 12 fabrics for Round 3*

$1/4$ yard of red fabrics for center squares

$1/4$-inch graph paper, at least 14 by 14 inches

Straightedge

2 yards of unbleached all-cotton muslin for foundation squares

Masking tape

Pins

Thread to blend

$7/8$ yard of striped denim (or other fabric) for block borders

Fabric scissors

$2 1/2$ yards of solid denim for sashing**

Denim sewing-machine needle

$1/2$ yard of fabric (can be scraps) for edges

Queen-size flat sheet for backing

Five buttons

SEWING WORKSHOP

Color Block Duvet Cover

BRIGHT FABRICS AND DENIM in this full-size duvet cover update a historic American quilt pattern known as Log Cabin. The pattern consists of strips of fabric, the "logs," surrounding a red center square that symbolizes the cabin's fireplace. In this version, denim borders set off and space out 12 colorful blocks, each one unique. You can buy half as many fabrics for the blocks if you make two of each block; you'll still need $1/4$ yard of red fabrics for the center squares. Prewash all fabrics.

FINISHED SIZE approximately $67 1/2$ by 88 inches

TIP

THE KEY TO SUCCESS WITH

THIS PATTERN IS TO CHOOSE

CONTRASTING FABRICS FOR

THE THREE "ROUNDS" OF

STRIPS IN THE COLOR BLOCKS.

BECAUSE FABRICS TEND TO

BLEND MORE WHEN CUT INTO

PIECES AND SEAMED, IT'S

BEST TO OPT FOR MORE,

RATHER THAN LESS, CONTRAST.

JUXTAPOSE LIGHT AND DARK

OR WARM AND COOL FABRICS

TO ACCENTUATE THE PATTERN.

*See Step 1 for an explanation of color-block "rounds." Fabrics for the Log Cabin blocks must measure at least 40 inches wide.

**The denim can measure 54 or 60 inches wide.

Cutting the Strips and Center Squares

1 For each color block, you'll need three "rounds" of same fabric strips; the rounds are shown in different colors below. Use the rotary cutting tools to cut the following strips for each block.

From the Round 1 fabric, cut pieces of these dimensions:
- 1½ by 3½ inches for Strip 1
- 1½ by 4½ inches for Strips 2 and 3
- 1½ by 5½ inches for Strip 4

From the Round 2 fabric, cut pieces of these dimensions:
- 2 by 5½ inches for Strip 5
- 2 by 7 inches for Strips 6 and 7
- 2 by 8½ inches for Strip 8

From the Round 3 fabric, cut pieces of these dimensions:
- 2½ by 8½ inches for Strip 9
- 2½ by 10½ inches for Strips 10 and 11
- 2½ by 12½ inches for Strip 12

The striped denim border around each block is added later.

From the red fabrics, cut 12 squares, each 3½ by 3½ inches.

Preparing the Foundation Squares

2 Copy the block illustration below onto graph paper, enlarging it to full scale. Number the strips as shown. Mark the center point with a pencil.

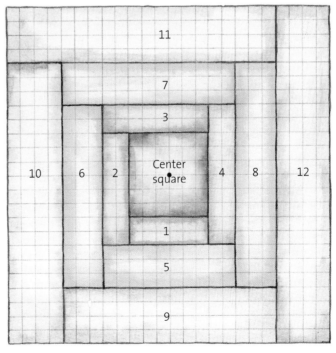

☐ = ½ inch

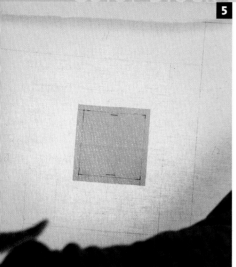

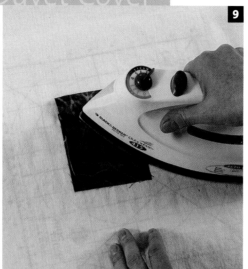

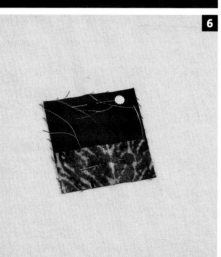

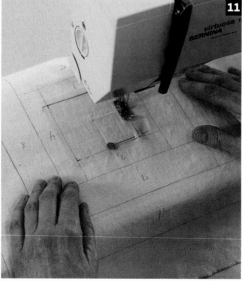

3 Tear the muslin into 12 squares, each 14 by 14 inches; these will be the foundation squares for the color blocks. Press the squares. Fold each square in half twice and press the folds in the middle to find the center point. Firmly mark the center point with a pencil so the point shows on the other side.

4 Tape the block pattern to a window. Tape a foundation square over the pattern, aligning the center points. Using a pencil and a straightedge, trace the block onto the muslin foundation. It's easiest to mark the beginning and end of each line with a dot, then connect the dots. Number all the strips.

Making the Blocks

5 With the marked side up, orient the foundation as shown in Step 2, so that Strip 1 is below the center square. (This placement is essential to the stitching order.) Turn the foundation to the unmarked side. Fold a red square in half, with right sides together. Fold it in half again; crease the folded point. Unfold the square. Put a pin through the center of the square, then into the center of the muslin. With these points aligned, pin the square to the foundation along two edges. Hold the foundation up to the light, with the muslin toward you, as shown, to make sure the red square extends exactly ¼ inch—no more, no less—beyond the marked lines. This step is important; if the alignment is off here, all the strips will be off.

6 Turn the foundation back to the unmarked side. Align one long raw edge of Strip 1 with the lower raw edge of the center square, right sides together. Make sure the ends and edges are also aligned. Pin.

7 Hold the foundation up to the light, with the marked side toward you, and check to see that the edges extend precisely ¼ inch beyond the marked lines.

8 On the marked side, stitch along the line shared by the center square and Strip 1. Start just a few stitches before the beginning of the line; end just a few stitches beyond the line.

9 Turn the foundation to the strip side. Fold back Strip 1 and press it against the seam allowances.

10 Align one long raw edge of Strip 2 with the left edge of the center square and the end of Strip 1, right sides together, as shown. Pin.

11 Turn the foundation to the marked side. Check to see that the edges extend precisely ¼ inch beyond the marked lines. Stitch along the line shared by the center square and Strip 2, beginning just

before the line and ending just after it, as with the first strip.

HINT: When you're assembling a color block, remember that the fabric strips always go on the *unmarked* side of the muslin foundation; you always sew on the *marked* side.

12 Turn the foundation to the fabric side. Fold back Strip 2 and press it against the seam allowances.

13 Align one long raw edge of Strip 3 with the edge of the center square and the end of Strip 2, right sides together. Pin.

14 Turn the foundation to the marked side. Check to see that the edges extend precisely ¼ inch beyond the marked lines. Stitch along the line shared by the center square and Strip 3, beginning just before the line and ending just after it.

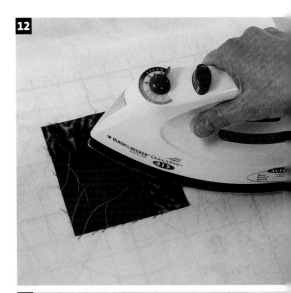

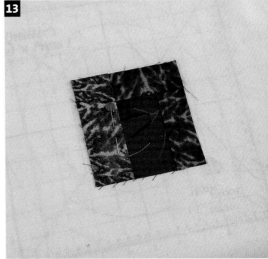

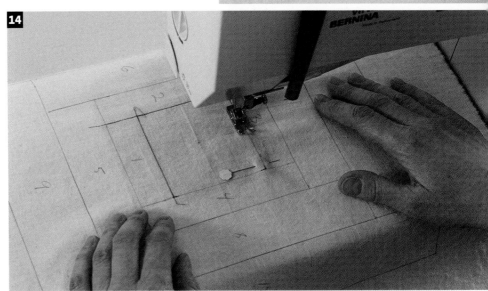

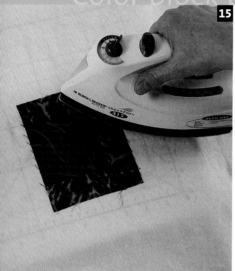

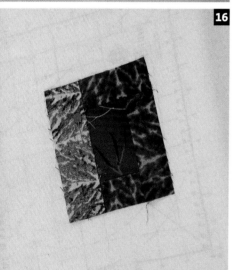

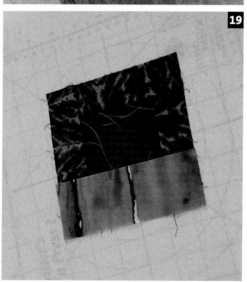

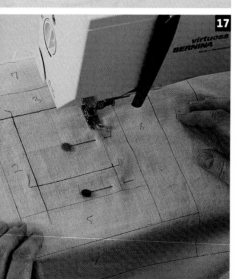

15 Turn the foundation to the fabric side. Fold back Strip 3 and press it against the seam allowances.

16 Align one long raw edge of Strip 4 with the edge of the center square and the ends of Strips 1 and 3, right sides together. Pin.

17 Turn the foundation to the marked side. Check to see that the edges extend precisely ¼ inch beyond the marked lines. Stitch along the line shared by the center square and Strip 4, beginning just before the line and ending just after it.

18 Turn the foundation to the fabric side. Fold back Strip 4 and press it against the seam allowances. You've now completed Round 1 of the block.

19 Align one long raw edge of Strip 5 with the edge of Strip 1 and the ends of Strips 2 and 4, right sides together. Pin, stitch, and press as you have the previous strips.

20 Add Strips 6, 7, and 8 to complete Round 2.

21 Add Strips 9, 10, 11, and 12 to complete Round 3. With the marked side up, pin the foundation and the color block together at the outer marked lines. Baste on the lines, pivoting at the corners. Turn the block over so the fabric side is up.

22 Use the rotary ruler and rotary cutter to trim the blocks ¼ inch beyond the basting. *Do not trim on the basting lines.*

23 Repeat Steps 4 through 22 to make a total of 12 blocks.

24 Lay out the blocks, three across and four down. Number the blocks with masking tape.

Adding the Block Borders

25 From the striped denim fabric, cut 16 strips, each 1¾ inches wide, across the width of the fabric. Sew a strip to one edge of a block, right sides together, using a ¼-inch seam allowance.

26 Fold back the strip and press it away from the block. Trim the ends of the strip flush with the edges of the block.

27 Stitch another strip to an adjoining edge of the block, including the end of the strip you just added. Fold back the strip and press it away from the block.

28 Trim the ends of the second strip flush with the edges of the block and the first strip.

29 Add the remaining strips in the same manner. Add border strips to the other color blocks.

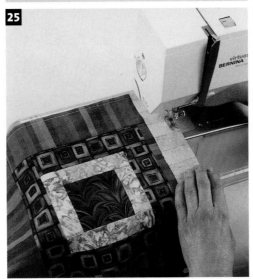

Adding the Denim Sashing and Borders

30 From the solid denim, cut the following lengthwise strips:
- Eight strips, each 6½ by 15 inches, for the vertical sashing pieces
- Three strips, each 6½ by 56 inches, for the horizontal sashing pieces
- Two strips, each 6½ inches by approximately 78 inches, for the side borders
- Two strips, each 6½ inches by approximately 70 inches, for the top and bottom borders

31 Lay out the upper-left block and a short sashing strip as shown.

32 Right sides together and raw edges aligned, pin and stitch the sashing strip to the right edge of the block, using a ¼-inch seam allowance.

33 Fold back the sashing strip and press it against the seam allowances.

34 Add the second block to the other edge of the sashing strip.

35 Add another sashing strip to the opposite edge of the second block, followed by the third block, to complete the top row. Position the first horizontal sashing strip below the first row, as shown.

36 Join the top row and the first horizontal sashing strip. Join the

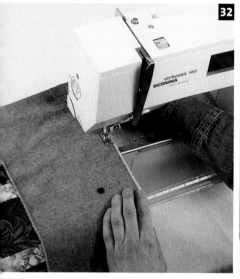

next three blocks and the vertical sashing strips to make the second row. Add the second row to the other edge of the horizontal sashing strip, lining up the seams on the vertical sashing strips from row to row.

37 Join the remaining blocks and sashing strips to complete the interior of the cover.

38 Lay out the cover and measure vertically through the center. Trim the side borders (the ones originally cut 78 inches long) to this length. Right sides together, add the side borders; fold back the borders and press them against the seam allowances.

39 Measure the cover horizontally through the center, including the just-added borders. Trim the top and bottom borders to this width. Right sides together, add the borders; fold back the borders and press them against the seam allowances.

Finishing the Duvet Cover

40 From the edging fabric, measure, mark, and cut eight 2-inch-wide crosswise strips (from selvage to selvage). Join the strips, using a ¼-inch seam allowance, to make one long strip. From this strip cut two strips the exact width of the cover top and two strips the exact length. Fold each strip in half lengthwise, wrong sides together, and press.

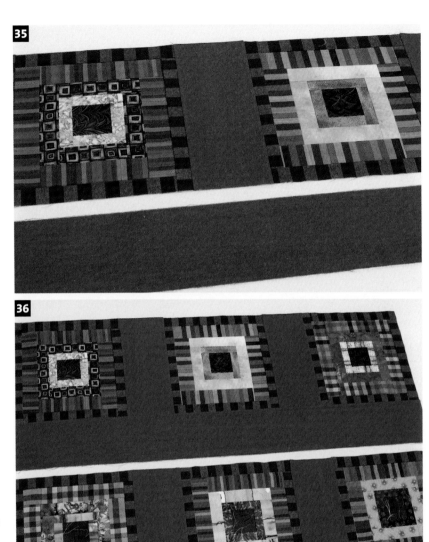

41 Open the ends of a strip and turn under a little more than ¼ inch; finger-press, then refold the strip. With right sides together and raw edges aligned, pin the folded strip to the corresponding edge on the cover top, starting a little more than ¼ inch from a corner; baste.

42 Repeat to join another strip to an adjoining edge. You should have a small square, slightly larger than ¼ inch, of the cover top show-

ing at the corner. Join strips to the remaining edges in the same way.

43 To attach the backing, see "Backing the Cover Top" on page 19.

MATERIALS

1-inch light-colored
painter's tape

Latex primer

1 quart of light blue
latex paint with satin
finish, for base coat

Standard paint roller
with low-nap cover
(¼ or ⅜ inch)

Paint tray

Three disposable
tray liners

Steel tape measure

Plumb line

Carpenter's level

36-inch
metal straightedge

1 quart of denim blue
latex paint with
semigloss finish

1 quart of
latex glazing medium

Gloves

Small paint roller
and low-nap cover
(¼ or ⅜ inch)

Texturing roller cover

2-inch tapered brush

Paint key or nail

IN A WEEKEND

Denim Walls

IT TAKES ONLY A FEW inexpensive paint tools, light and dark blue paint, and glazing medium to create the look of patchwork denim squares. A slight overlapping of paint where the squares meet creates the look of seams. Because the effect is so striking, you'll probably want to limit it to one wall, as was done in this attic playroom. If you like, add upholsterer's tacks to the corners where the squares meet, to suggest the rivets in blue jeans.

TIP

TEXTURING ROLLER COVERS
HAVE LITTLE LOOPS ON
THE SURFACE THAT PRODUCE
A DEFINITE DIRECTIONAL
PATTERN, OR NAP. EXPERIMENT
WITH A TEXTURING ROLLER
COVER AND PAINT ON YOUR
WALL OR ON A PIECE OF
WALLBOARD TO DECIDE
WHICH WAY TO SNAP THE
COVER ONTO THE ROLLER.
ALWAYS ROLL IN THE SAME
DIRECTION, NOT FORWARD
AND BACKWARD.

Preparing and Marking the Wall

1 Tape the wall edges, window frame, and ceiling line. Prime the wall and paint it light blue.

2 Find the horizontal midpoint of the wall and, with a helper, drop a plumb line from the ceiling at that point. Mark the center line on the wall with a pencil.

3 Determine the square size. If your wall has a window, use the measurement from the bottom of the windowsill to the top of the baseboard for the square size so you'll have a row of complete squares from the window to the baseboard. If your wall has no window, choose a square size that divides evenly into your ceiling height. Using the steel tape, measure and mark off the squares, starting from the center line.

4 Using the level and straight-edge, draw the vertical and horizontal lines for the squares.

5 Tape off every other square, placing the tape on the outside of the pencil lines and pressing it firmly against the lines. You will paint these squares first. Put small pieces of tape in the alternate squares to avoid painting them by mistake.

4a

4b

5

Painting the Wall

6 Mix the denim blue paint and glazing medium in a 1:1 ratio. Using the small roller and low-nap cover, apply the paint-and-glaze mixture to the taped-off squares.

7 Using the standard roller and texturing roller cover, go over the paint vertically to create the look of denim. Roll in one direction only—either up or down.

8 When the paint is dry to the touch, remove all the tape. On the light blue squares, apply the paint-and-glaze mixture with the small roller and low-nap cover.

9 Where the squares meet, slightly overlap the edges of the just-painted squares to create the illusion of seams.

10 Using the standard roller and texturing roller cover, go over the paint horizontally, rolling in one direction only.

11 At the wall edges and the ceiling line, apply the paint-and-glaze mixture with a 2-inch tapered brush. Use a paint key or nail to mimic the effect of the texturing roller cover, moving it in the same direction as the paint grain, horizontally or vertically, depending on which square you're in. Allow the paint to dry.

MATERIALS

Trisodium phosphate, available at home centers and hardware stores

¾-inch blue painter's tape

Latex primer

Standard paint roller and low-nap roller cover (¼ or ⅜ inch)

Extended handle for paint roller

Latex paint for floor

2-inch paintbrush

Paint tray

Eight disposable tray liners

12-inch vinyl floor tiles for color placement, available at home centers and flooring stores

180-grit sandpaper (optional)

Small paint roller and low-nap roller cover (¼ or ⅜ inch)

Latex paint in six colors for squares

IN A WEEKEND

Scattered-squares Floor

PAINTING YOUR FLOOR is an easy, inexpensive alternative to installing traditional floor coverings. You can prime and paint both plywood and oriented strand board subflooring. If the joints are uneven, use leveling floor compound, available at home centers; follow the manufacturer's instructions carefully, sanding the surface before you prime and paint. Countersink nails or screws, if necessary. In a high-traffic room, apply two coats of water-based polyurethane to protect the surface.

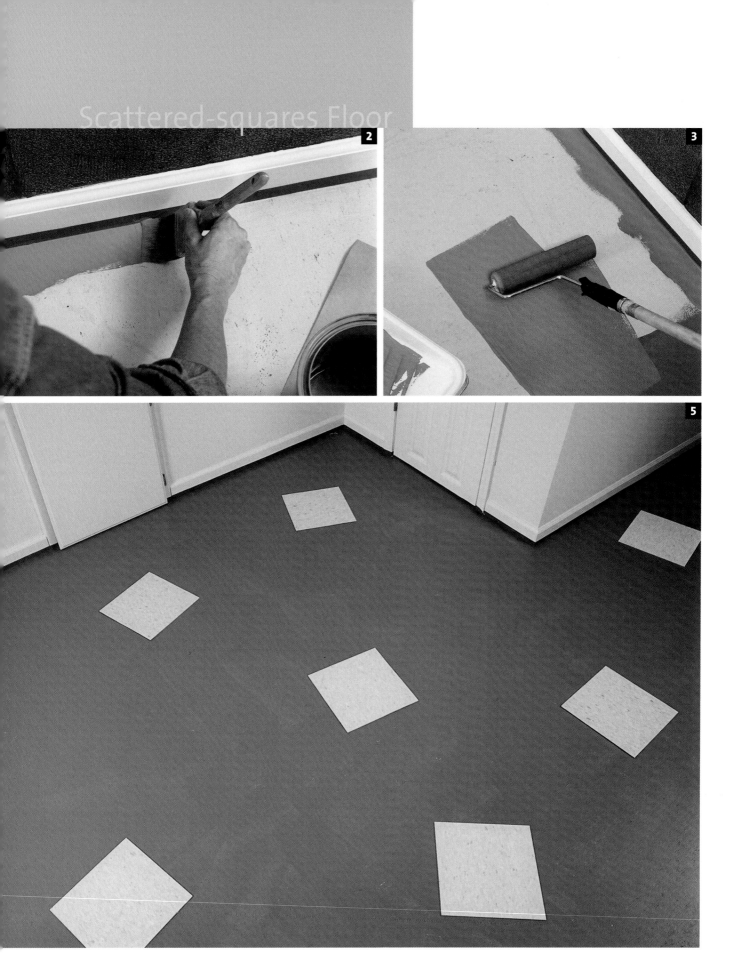

Preparing and Painting the Floor

1 Wash the floor with trisodium phosphate. Tape off the baseboards using blue painter's tape, then prime the floor, starting at one end of the room and using the paint roller with the long handle.

2 "Cut in" the floor paint at the edges, using the 2-inch paintbrush, as shown.

3 Using the paint roller with the long handle, roll paint over the floor. Allow to dry; apply a second coat.

4 When the second coat is dry to the touch, remove the tape from the baseboards.

Painting the Squares

5 "Scatter" the tiles on the floor, varying their angles and the spacing between them.

6 Tape around each tile, creating a square. Remove the tiles.

7 Lightly sand each taped-off square or wash with trisodium phosphate prior to painting. Using the small roller, paint each square. Allow to dry; paint a second coat. Lighter colors may require a third coat.

8 When the paint is dry to the touch, remove the tape.

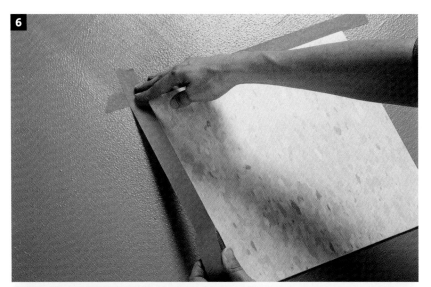

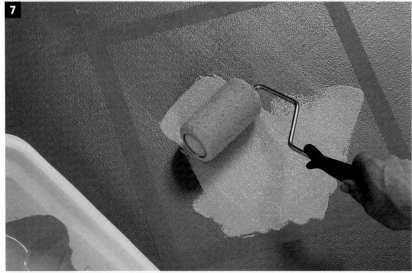

Fabric scissors

6- by 24-inch rotary ruler, available at quilt shops and fabric stores

4¾ yards of denim, 60 inches wide

3¼ yards of quilt batting, 90 inches wide

6½ yards of muslin, at least 42 inches wide

Pins

Thread to blend

Four skeins of #3 red perle cotton thread

Large-eyed embroidery needle

Four 25- by 4-inch foam cushion forms

Four 33-gallon plastic garbage bags

SEWING WORKSHOP

Boxed Floor Cushions

THESE BOXED CUSHIONS make great extra seating in a playroom; stacked, they function like a small table or work surface. The key to perfectly square cushions is to line up the corners on the top and bottom squares with the boxing strip that joins the squares and encircles the foam form. Bright red handstitching trims the edges and creates the custom look of welt.

FINISHED SIZE

four cushions,

each 26½ inches square

by 5½ inches high

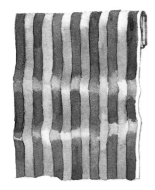

TIP

THE FOAM CUSHION FORMS
SHOWN HERE ARE 25 INCHES
SQUARE, BUT YOU MAY NEED
SMALLER FORMS IF YOUR
FABRIC IS LESS THAN 60
INCHES WIDE. TO DETERMINE
THE SIZE OF THE FORMS,
DIVIDE THE USABLE FABRIC
WIDTH (EXCLUDING THE
SELVAGES) BY 2 (FOR THE TOP
AND BOTTOM SQUARES OF
FABRIC), THEN SUBTRACT 2½
INCHES (FOR SEAM ALLOWANCES
AND WELT). THAT'S THE SIZE
FOAM FORM TO BUY.

Cutting the Pieces

1 From the denim cut eight strips, each 6½ inches by the *width* of the fabric; trim the selvages. Cut eight squares, each 27½ by 27½ inches.

From the batting cut four strips, each 6½ inches by the *length* of the batting; and eight squares, each 27½ by 27½ inches.

From the muslin cut two strips, each 6½ inches by the *length* of the fabric; and eight squares, each 27½ by 27½ inches. Cut the muslin strips in half crosswise, to make four strips.

Basting the Pieces

2 Layer a muslin square, batting square, and denim square, right side up. Pin and baste ¼ inch from the edges. Repeat to make eight fabric-and-batting "sandwiches."

3 Join two denim strips, using a ¼-inch seam allowance, to make one long strip for each cushion. Press the seam allowances open.

4 Layer a muslin strip, batting strip, and joined denim strip, right side up. Trim the denim even with the muslin and batting. Pin and baste as you did the squares to make a boxing strip. (These are called boxing strips because they give the cushions their square appearance.) Repeat to four boxing strips.

Making the Cushions

5 Denim sides together, place one end of a boxing strip at one corner of a square, with the edges aligned. Pin the strip to the edge of the square. Using a ½-inch seam allowance, start stitching ½ inch from the end of the strip; backstitch to secure the beginning stitches, then continue stitching to ½ inch from the next corner; backstitch to secure the stitches.

6 Take the piece out from under the needle and clip into the seam allowance at the point where you stopped stitching. Make sure the clip is perpendicular to the stitching.

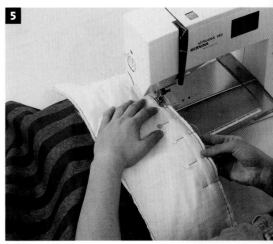

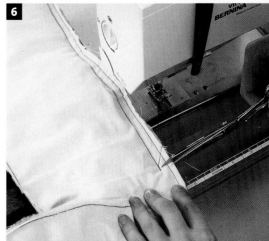

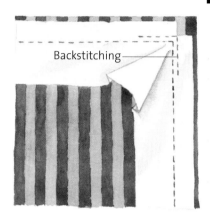

Backstitching

7 Pull the boxing strip around to the adjoining edge of the square, opening up the clip. Put the piece under the needle and resume stitching, starting at the clip. Backstitch to secure the stitches.

8 Pin and stitch down the side.

9 Continue stitching around the square, clipping and pivoting at the corners. Leave the middle of one edge open approximately 15 inches to insert the cushion form; backstitch at the start and finish of the opening to prevent the stitching from ripping when you insert the form later.

10 Stop stitching ½ inch short of the corner where you started (fold back the strip so it doesn't get caught in the stitching); backstitch. Remove the piece from under the needle and lay it flat on

your work surface. Trim the end of the boxing strip even with the square and rebaste the layers at the trimmed end.

11 Bring the ends of the strips together, denim against denim, pulling the square out of the way. Pin the strips at the point where the stitching stops.

12 Pin the ends of the strips together. Using a ½-inch seam allowance, start stitching the ends ½ inch from the long, unstitched edge of the boxing strip; backstitch to secure. Stitch to the pin you placed in Step 11 and backstitch.

13 Pin another fabric-and-batting square to the free edge of the boxing strip, denim against denim, making sure any stripes are running in the same direction on both squares. Carefully align the

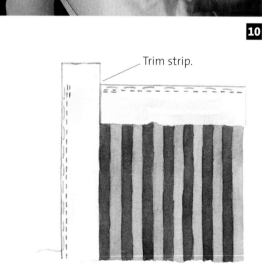

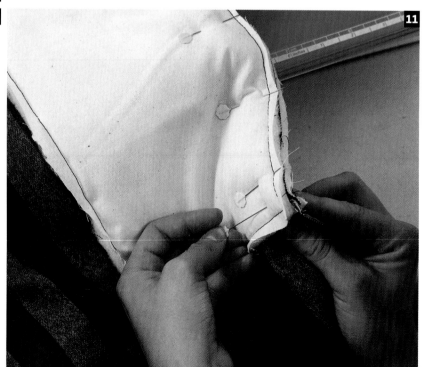

Trim strip.

corners with those on the first square. Stitch each edge as you did in Steps 5 through 7, stopping short of the corner and clipping into the seam allowance. Do not leave an opening.

Finishing the Cushions

14 Turn the cushion cover right side out. Work the fabric to the edges and corners. Using the red perle cotton thread and the large-eyed needle, "stab-stitch" about ¾ inch from the edges (insert the needle straight up and down through the layers, making very short stitches), leaving the edge with the opening unstitched.

15 To help ease the foam form into the cover, put the form in a plastic bag and slip it into the cover through the opening, bending the corners of the foam as needed. Reach into the cover and rip the plastic bag on one side; work the bag around the foam and out through the opening.

16 Slipstitch the opening closed. Stab-stitch the remaining edge with the perle cotton thread.

17 Repeat Steps 5 through 16 to make a total of four cushions.

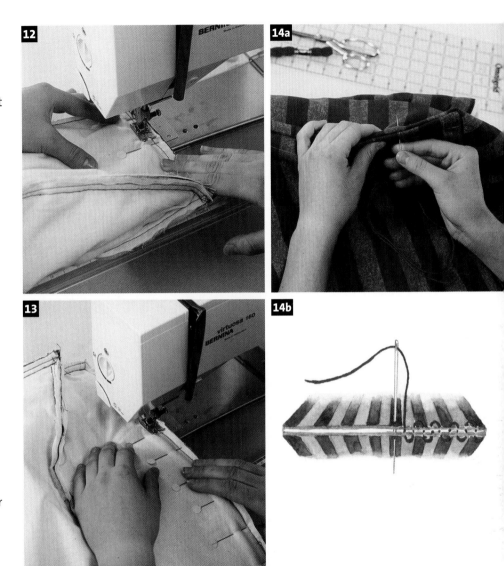

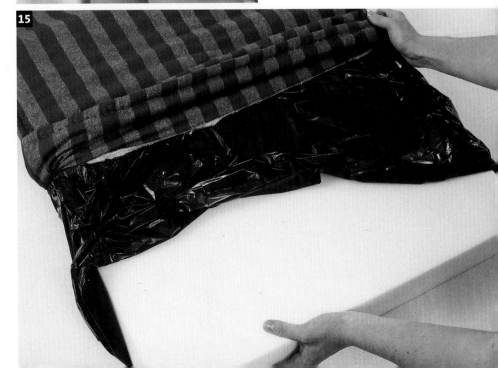

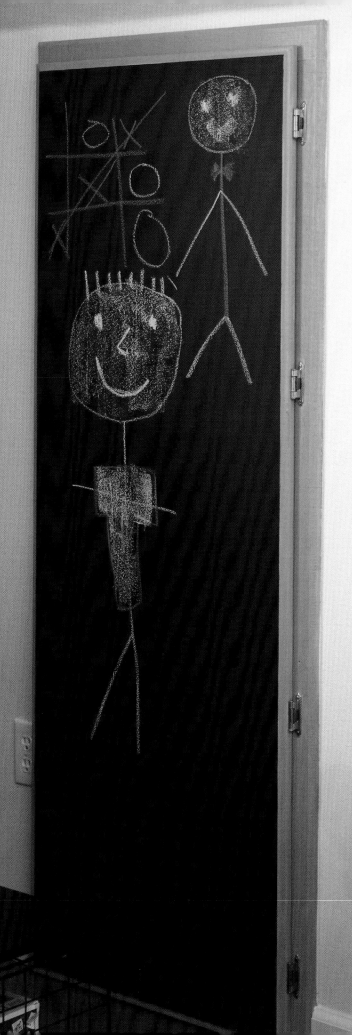

Just for
Fun

Chalk It Up

FACING PAGE: Blackboard paint turned plain cupboard doors into practical writing and drawing surfaces. Bright yellow-orange paint on the trim outlines the doors and adds a bit of intense color to the white walls.

Clutter Control

ABOVE: Stackable wire-storage units come as flat components; you snap them together to form the cubes. Plastic bins slide in and out for easy access.

Scooter Stools

BELOW: Inexpensive rolling stools from an automotive supply store provide extra seating—and allow the host and guests to race from square to square.

Bendable Floor Lamp

ABOVE: Primary-colored glass shades on flexible arms give this floor lamp its whimsical, sculptural appeal and entice young guests to rearrange the elements.

Outer Limits

THE SPIRIT OF ADVENTURE emanates from every corner of this reinvented attic bedroom. Deep, dark colors portray the night sky on the alcove wall and sloping ceiling; night turns to day on an adjoining wall decorated with astronomical charts, symbolic of early exploration. Down-to-earth projects include a high-tech-looking desk made of tool chests and a laminate counter, a cargo bedspread trimmed with grommets and carabiners, and comfy polar fleece accessories. Everyone's favorite feature, hands down, is the gleaming metal wall (see page 79), which serves as a magnetic bulletin board and backdrop for a child's dreams.

"Night and day" describes the difference between the room before and after. Paint and fabric were the main decorating ingredients.

MATERIALS

1¼ yards of polar
fleece, 60 inches wide,
for *each* pillow sham

Tailor's or quilter's
chalk marker

Fabric scissors

Thread

Five standard-size
bed pillows

Pins

6- by 24-inch
rotary ruler, available
at fabric stores and
quilt shops

2 yards of
polar fleece, 60 inches
wide, for throw

DO IT TODAY

Pillow Shams and Throw

PLUSH PILLOWS and a fringed throw, all stitched from polar fleece, make this bed a cozy spot to read and relax. Ordinary bed pillows fill the envelope-style pillow shams; "yarn" made from strips of fleece embellishes the flanges. The fleece throw (see page 77) folds neatly into a square that slips into an attached pillow sack. When the throw is unfolded, the empty sack is the perfect place to warm cold toes.

FINISHED SIZE

pillows: approximately

20 by 37 inches

(including flanges)

throw: 60 by 72 inches

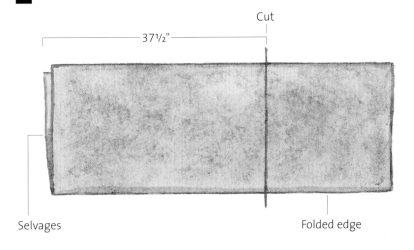

1

Cut

37½"

Selvages

Folded edge

Cutting and Pinning the Pieces

1 For each sham, fold 1¼ yards of polar fleece in half crosswise (right or wrong sides together) and mark a chalk line 37½ inches from one selvage, as shown above. Cut along the line through both thicknesses. Set aside the leftover pieces from two of the shams for the front and back of the throw's pillow sack (see page 77). Use the other leftovers to make the "yarn" trim for the flanges in the next step.

2 To make the yarn, cut ½-inch-wide strips of fleece from the width of the leftover pieces. With your machine set on a long, wide zigzag stitch, sew down the middle of each strip, holding it taut with one hand in front and one in back. Set the strips aside. (You'll attach them to the flanges in Step 9.)

3 Center a pillow on the right side of one of the fleece pieces as shown below. Fold the fleece over the long sides of the pillow and pull it snug, overlapping the edges.

2

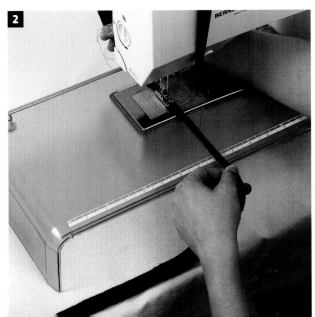

3

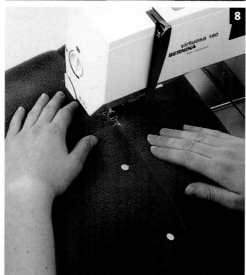

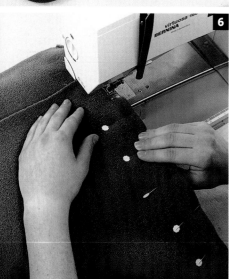

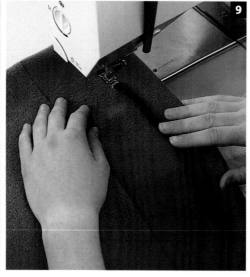

4 Pin the overlapping edges of the fleece at the center and at each end, making sure the overlap is the same on both ends. Carefully remove the pillow.

5 Pin across each end, through all layers of fleece.

Stitching the Shams

6 Stitch each end using a ¼-inch seam allowance. Turn the sham right side out.

7 Using the rotary ruler, measure and mark a chalk line 4¾ inches from the edge on each end.

8 Pin and stitch through all layers on the marked lines to create the flanges.

Finishing the Shams

9 Lay the fleece yarn strips made in Step 2 on the flanges and arrange them to make a design. Using a long, wide zigzag stitch, attach the strips to the flanges. Trim as needed.

10 Insert the pillow into the pillow sham through the envelope closure on the back.

11 Repeat Steps 3 through 10 for each additional pillow.

Hemming and Fringing the Throw

1 Using the 2 yards of polar fleece, fold in each long edge ³/₈ inch and stitch to make narrow hems.

2 Along each unhemmed edge, measure and mark a chalk line 3 inches from the raw edge. Using fabric scissors, cut ¹/₂-inch-wide fringe, stopping at the chalk line.

3 Set your machine on a long, wide zigzag stitch. Position the first piece of fringe under the needle at the chalk line. Start stitching down the middle of the fringe, backstitch to secure, then continue stitching, holding onto the fringe at the end and stretching it slightly.

4 When you can no longer hold onto the strip, backstitch and pull the threads and fringe out of the way and begin stitching again at the top of the next strip. When you've stitched all the fringe, trim the ends and the threads. Repeat to stitch the fringe at the other end of the throw.

Attaching the Pillow Sack

5 From the leftover sham pieces (see Step 1 on page 75), cut two squares, each 18 by 18 inches. Right sides together and raw edges aligned, pin and stitch the pieces around the edges using a ¹/₄-inch seam allowance and leaving a 10-inch opening on one edge. Turn the piece right side out and slipstitch the opening closed.

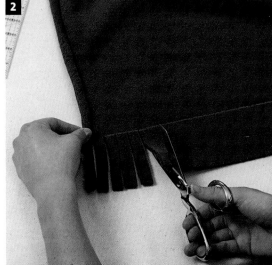

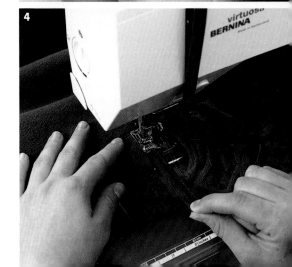

6 Using other leftovers, make fleece yarn (see Step 2 on page 75) and attach it to one side of the sewn square using a long, wide zigzag stitch.

7 On the right side of the throw, center the square, decorated side down, along one fringed edge; make sure the edge of the square aligns with the base of the fringe, as shown. Pin the square to the throw along all the edges.

8 Topstitch the square to the throw on three of the pinned edges, leaving the edge toward the center of the throw unstitched. Remove the pins.

Folding the Throw

9 To fit the throw into the pillow sack, first lay the throw on the bed with the square facedown. Fold the throw into thirds lengthwise (a). Next, fold the throw over itself, toward the square (b), ending with the folded throw on top of the square (c). (It may take several attempts to get it right.) Turn the entire throw over, still folded (d). Reach into the square to the corners, grab the throw through all layers, and turn the square inside out, encasing the throw and forming a pillow (e).

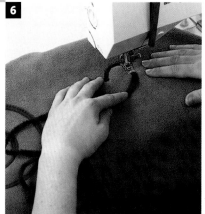

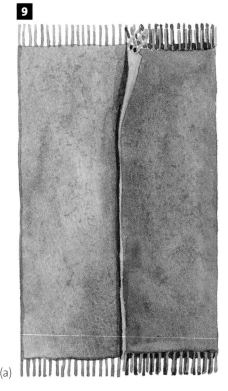

(a)

(b)

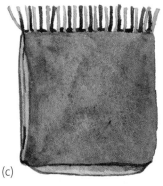

(c)

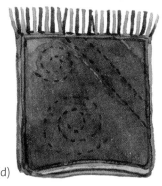

(d)

(e)

MATERIALS

Steel measuring tape

Stud finder

Chalk line

Plywood scrap

Leather gloves

24-gauge galvanized
sheet metal,
cut to fit your wall
(see the tip on page 81)

Electric drill
and ³/₁₆-inch drill bit

#8 self-tapping
metal screws,
1¼ inches long

Soffit vent strips, cut
to fit your panels
(see the tip on page 81)

#8 flathead screws,
1¼ inches long

IN A WEEKEND

Metal Wall

THIS DAZZLING YET SIMPLE wall treatment consists of sheets of galvanized metal screwed to the wall, with inexpensive vent strips covering the seams. Standard magnets hold anything and everything (including these clocks) to the surface. The metal sheets are available through sheet-metal suppliers; they can vary widely in appearance, so ask for ones that look similar. They also look different on each side, giving you a choice of finishes. You can attach the sheets to any wall surface, as long as you screw through the metal and into the studs.

TIP

ALWAYS WEAR LEATHER

GLOVES WHEN YOU

WORK WITH SHEET-METAL

PANELS; THE EDGES

ARE EXTREMELY SHARP.

79

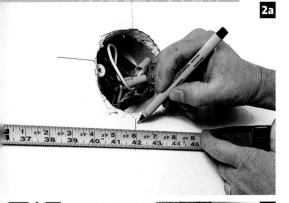

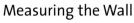

Measuring the Wall

1 Remove any light fixtures and outlet covers or switch plates from the wall.

2 Carefully measure and mark each fixture or outlet opening as follows:
A. Measure and mark horizontal and vertical lines through the center of the opening.
B. Measure from the right edge of the wall to the vertical marked line. At the floor, measure from the top of the baseboard to the horizontal marked line.
C. Also measure the size of the opening.

3 Make a sketch of your wall, including the precise measurements for fixtures and outlets; give this sketch to the sheet-metal worker when you have the panels cut. Be sure to explain what the panels are for so the metal worker will make the tidiest possible cuts.

4 Using the stud finder, mark the studs at the very top and bottom of the wall.

5 Measure and mark the precise midpoint on the wall. If you'll be attaching an odd number of panels, plan to install the middle panel first, centered exactly on the wall's midpoint. For an even number, plan to install the panel to the right of the midpoint first. For either installation, snap a chalk line on the wall to mark the right-hand edge of the first panel.

Attaching the Panels

6 Protect your work surface with a plywood scrap. Then predrill holes at the top and bottom of each panel at intervals corresponding to the wall studs, measuring from center to center. (Note: This room has a recessed ledge at the top of the wall, with a horizontal header that allowed the homeowner to screw into the header at even intervals. Standard walls don't have headers, so you'll need to attach the panels to the studs.)

8

THE METAL PANELS COME IN
3- BY 10-FOOT OR 4- BY 10-
FOOT SHEETS. YOU'LL MOUNT
THEM VERTICALLY, SO IF THE
WIDTH OF YOUR WALL DOES
NOT DIVIDE EVENLY INTO
3- OR 4-FOOT INCREMENTS
(AND IT PROBABLY WON'T),
YOU'LL NEED TO HAVE ONE
SHEET TRIMMED TO FIT AND
PLACE IT AT ONE END OF
THE WALL OR HAVE ALL THE
SHEETS TRIMMED TO EQUAL
WIDTHS THAT ADD UP TO
YOUR TOTAL WALL WIDTH.
HAVE THE LENGTHS TRIMMED
AS NEEDED TO START THE
PANELS ABOVE THE BASE-
BOARD. HAVE THE VENT
STRIPS CUT TO MATCH THE
PANEL LENGTH.

7 With a helper, position the middle (or right-of-midpoint) panel so its right edge aligns with the chalk line you marked in Step 5. Using the self-tapping metal screws, attach the panel to the wall at the top and bottom.

8 Using the marks you made for the studs, snap chalk lines on top of the panel as guides for the screws that will go into each stud.

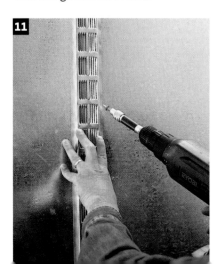

11

9 Working from the top down, predrill holes through the metal and into the studs along the chalk lines at intervals of 2 feet. Install the screws.

10 Position and attach the remaining panels in the same way.

Attaching the Vent Strips

11 On your work surface, predrill holes in the vent strips at 2-foot intervals, adjusting the intervals as necessary to avoid any existing screws near the panel seams. Holding a vent strip over a panel seam, predrill into the panels; attach the vent strips and panels with the flathead screws.

81

MAKEOVER MAGIC

Paint the Sky

A CHILD'S PASSION for space and exploration guided this decorative painting plan. A green-and-purple mariner's compass and old astronomical
charts float against a golden backdrop on one wall; to the left, the night sky
spills out of the alcove and up the sloping ceiling (see pages 72 and 73). You
don't need experience or special tools to create these effects, but it's wise to
practice first on pieces of primed and painted plywood or hardboard.

Painting the Compass Wall

1 Using blue painter's tape, tape the baseboards and window frames on the compass wall; also tape the edges of the sky wall or walls. Prime the compass wall if necessary. Paint with the pale yellow latex paint; allow the paint to dry. Apply a second coat if needed.

2 Using the yardstick and a pencil, draw the compass lines on the wall. The schematic on page 84 shows the shape and dimensions of this compass. Adjust the scale to suit your wall size.

3 With a small craft brush and the green acrylic paint, paint half of each compass arm, starting at the pencil lines and working inward. Strive for an uneven quality to the color. Leave "chips" and "cracks" in the color to suggest age.

4 Paint the other half of each compass arm with purple acrylic paint.

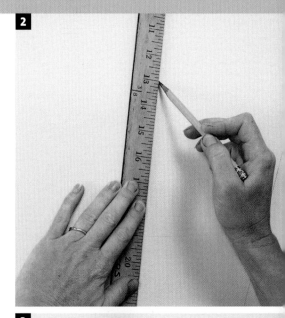

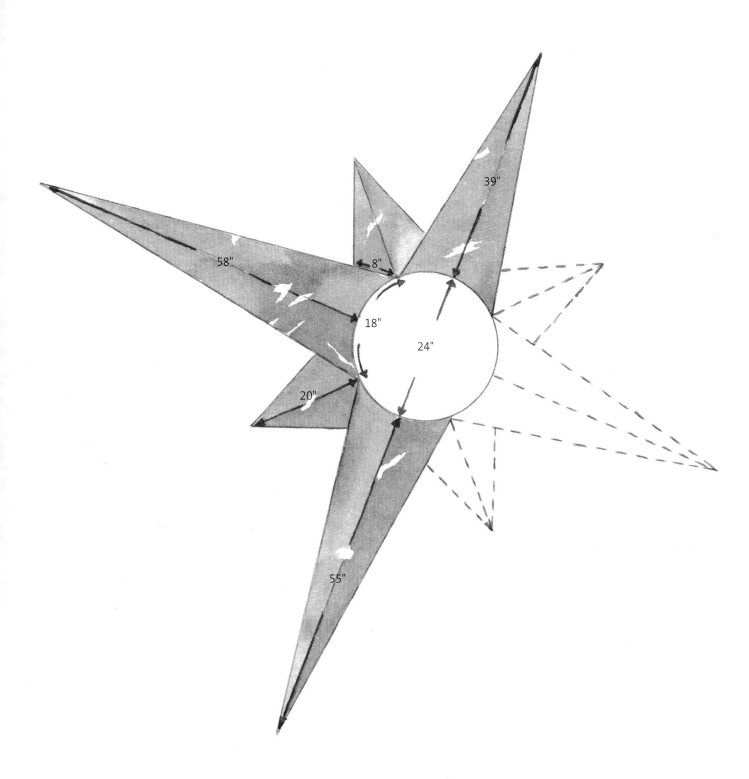

39"

58"

8"

18"

24"

20"

55"

Mariner's compass. See Step 2 on page 83.

5 Partially mix 1 part orange acrylic paint and 1 part glazing medium in a plastic bowl. Wet a sponge and wring out some, but not all, of the water. Dip the sponge into the paint mixture, then dab the paint onto the wall in an up-and-down motion, all around the compass to the wall edges.

6 With your hand in a plastic bag, blot the edges of the color to soften them. (You can also use a clean part of the sponge to work the color in.) Allow the paint to dry.

7 To add the astronomical charts, use the yardstick and a pencil to draw the straight lines and a pencil tied to string to draw the arcs. Paint the lines with charcoal gray and burgundy red acrylic paint; allow to dry.

8 With a damp sponge, apply a little of the pale yellow latex paint onto the wall in an up-and-down motion and work it in using either method described in Step 6.

9 Sponge the paint over the compass and charts sparingly.

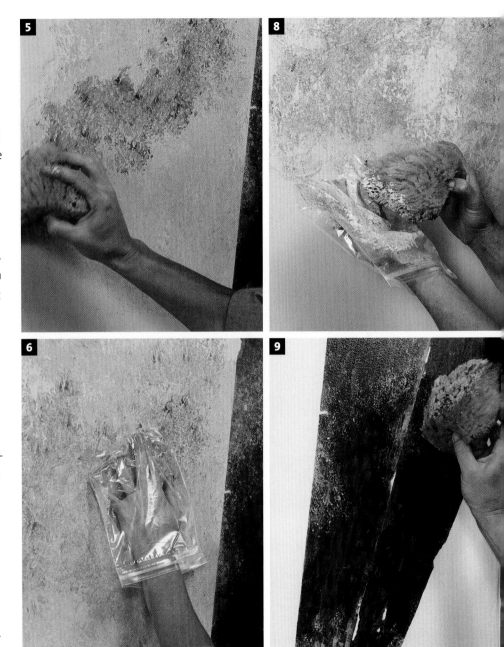

TIP

HIGH VISCOSITY ACRYLIC PHTHALO GREEN

HIGH VISCOSITY ACRYLIC PRISM VIOLET

BY ONLY PARTIALLY MIXING THE ACRYLIC PAINT AND GLAZING MEDIUM IN STEP 5, YOU'LL GET SMALL BITS OF STRONGER COLOR WHEN YOU SPONGE THE WALL, GIVING THE OVERALL COLOR ADDED DIMENSION.

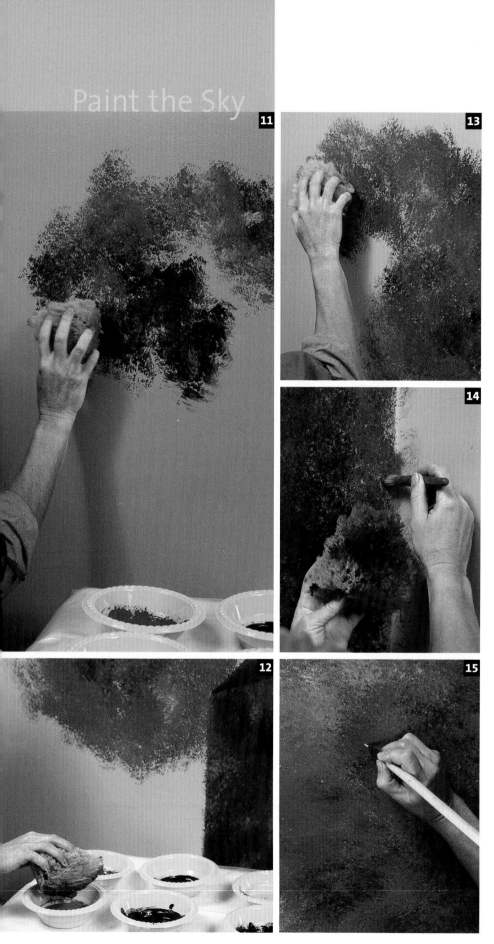

Painting the Sky Wall

10 Using blue painter's tape, tape the baseboards and window frames on the sky wall or walls; also tape the edges of the compass wall. Prime the sky wall with the latex primer if necessary. Paint with the light blue latex paint; allow the paint to dry.

11 In separate bowls, mix the dark blue, green, and purple acrylic paints with glazing medium. Using the dark blue mixture and a damp sponge, dab the paint onto the wall in an up-and-down motion, leaving areas of light blue background.

12 Using the same sponge, dip into a second color—purple, in this step—then dab randomly over the first areas of color.

13 Continue sponging outward, adding and mixing the colors on the wall. As you work over larger and larger areas, connect masses of the same colors to avoid creating isolated patches.

14 When you come to a corner, dip the stencil brush into the paint on the sponge and dab the brush onto the wall to continue the mottled effect. Allow the paint to dry.

15 Using the calligraphy brush and the gold acrylic paint straight from the tube, paint individual stars in the sky.

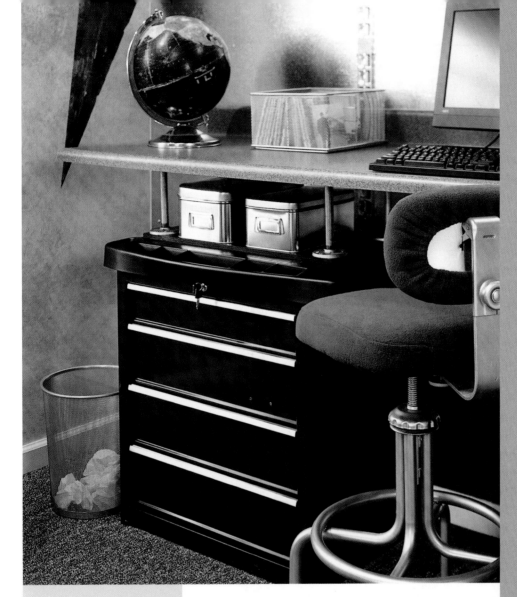

MATERIALS

Laminate top in desired
length (see the tip on
page 89), available at
home centers

Iron

Two trim kits
for laminate ends

Sandpaper

Latex primer

Two pieces of ¾-inch
plywood, cut to fit
the trays in the tops of
the tool chests

Paintbrush

Latex paint

Electric drill

Sixty-four wood screws,
¾ inch long

Sixteen galvanized
½-inch pipe flanges

Eight galvanized
½-inch double-threaded
pipe pieces,
each 10 inches long

Two tool chests*

Stud finder

Three L-brackets, with
screws appropriate for
your wall surface

*You can remove the
casters that come
on tool chests for a
slightly lower desk that
will not move.

IN A WEEKEND

Tool Chest Desk

AN INEXPENSIVE LAMINATE top and real tool chests make up this impressive desk unit. The construction couldn't be simpler: pieces of pipe connect the laminate to black-painted plywood bases, which fit into the shallow trays atop the chests (if the tool chests you buy don't have trays, you'll need to screw through the plywood and into the tops). Although the desk will be outgrown over time, the chests can go with their young owner (or to Dad's workshop) when he or she leaves home.

FINISHED SIZE 8 feet long, 25½ inches wide, 40 inches tall

Finishing the Laminate

1 Lay the laminate upside down. Using an iron and following the manufacturer's instructions, attach a piece of trim to each end of the laminate. (You can use the upside-down laminate as your work surface for Steps 3 and 4.)

Making the Plywood-and-Pipe Support Units

2 Sand and prime the plywood pieces. Paint both sides and the edges of each piece with the latex paint.

3 Using the drill and screws, attach a pipe flange to each corner of each plywood piece, aligning the edges of the flange with the edges of the plywood. Screw a piece of pipe into each flange.

4 Screw another flange onto the opposite end of each pipe.

Attaching the Support Units to the Laminate

5 Set the chests against the wall, with enough space between them for a desk chair. Next, place the pipe-and-plywood support units on top of the chests, plywood surfaces down and unattached flanges up. With the aid of a helper, center the laminate from side to side on top of the support units, flush with the back of the chests.

6 Reach under the laminate and carefully draw around each upper flange onto the laminate underside. Identify each support unit with a piece of tape marked "left" or "right" and indicate which is the front edge.

7 Remove the laminate and the support units. Turn the laminate upside down. Turn each support unit upside down so the flanges match the circles you drew in the previous step. Using a pencil, mark through the holes in the flanges onto the laminate.

8 At the marks, predrill holes for the screws. Reposition the support units and screw them to the laminate.

9 Flip the laminate over; rest the plywood bases in the chests' trays.

Securing the Desk to the Wall

10 Locate and mark the wall studs. Screw the L-brackets to the underside of the laminate, spacing them to correspond to the studs. Screw to the wall to secure.

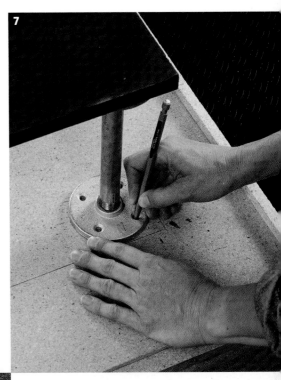

TIP

LAMINATE TOPS ARE SOLD BY LENGTH IN 2-FOOT INCREMENTS, FROM 4 FEET TO 12 FEET, IN A WIDE RANGE OF COLORS. THE STANDARD WIDTH IS 25 INCHES. MATCHING TRIM KITS FOR THE ENDS ARE SOLD SEPARATELY; EACH TRIM PIECE COMES WITH GLUE ALREADY APPLIED TO THE BACK.

MATERIALS

Flexible tape measure

5 yards of yellow
brushed cotton twill,
60 inches wide

Fabric scissors

Four safety pins

Tailor's or quilter's
chalk marker

2½ yards of olive green
mini-quilted cotton,
60 inches wide

Pins

Thread to blend or
contrast

6- by 24-inch
rotary ruler, available
at fabric stores and
quilt shops

Sixteen 1½-inch
grommets

Grommet set

Hammer

Four carabiners*

*"Carabiner" is the
name given to a type
of hook used by
mountain climbers.
The non-weight-bearing
versions shown here,
available at hardware
stores, are not intended
for that purpose. You
can use either type for
this project.

SEWING WORKSHOP

Cargo Bedspread

THE BED IS SUITED for a journey in a cargo-style bedspread. Trim and tailored, it's a crisp counterpoint to the dramatic skyscape, yet it repeats the yellow and green colors in the compass wall, linking the two halves of the room. Assembling the spread is easier than it looks; review the piecing layouts on the facing page to get a feel for the sequence of steps.

FINISHED SIZE queen size, 60 by 80 inches (top dimensions only, including trim), with a 12½-inch drop on the sides and foot

TIP

BRUSHED COTTON TWILL FABRIC HAS A DEFINITE DIRECTIONAL "NAP," WHICH AFFECTS THE LOOK OF THE FABRIC. IT DOESN'T MATTER WHICH WAY THE NAP GOES, AS LONG AS YOU CUT THE PIECES SO THE NAP IS CONSISTENT ON THE SPREAD TOP, FOOT DROP, AND SIDE DROPS.

Measuring and Cutting the Pieces

1 For this bed, the "drops" (the foot and side pieces) were cut 15 inches long, from the top to the bottom of the drop. To customize the spread for your child's bed, measure from the top edge of the bed to the point where you want the spread to end; add 2½ inches (for a ½-inch seam allowance and a 2-inch hem) to arrive at the cut width.

2 From the cotton twill, cut the following:
- One piece, 55 by 83½ inches, for the spread top
- Two pieces, each 15* by 83½ inches, for the side drops
- One piece, 15* by 55 inches, for the foot drop
- Two pieces, each 12 by 15* inches, for the tongues (the corner flaps at the foot of the bed)

Replace 15 with the length you determined in Step 1.

3 With safety pins, mark the head end of the spread top, the head end of each side drop, and the upper edge of the foot drop. Also label each side drop "right" or "left" with the tailor's chalk.

4 From the mini-quilted cotton, cut the following strips:
- Two strips, each 4 by 83½ inches, to trim the sides of the top
- One strip, 4 by 55 inches, to trim the foot of the top
- Eight strips, each 4 by 13½** inches, to trim the drops

**Replace 13½ with the cut length of your drop, minus 1½ inches.*

Making the Spread

NOTE: Use a ½-inch seam allowance throughout. See Step 1 on page 103 to make a seam guide.

5 Refer to the sewing layout below for the following steps.

5

(a)

Spread top

Green strip

(b)
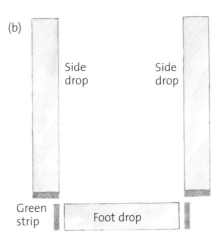
Side drop

Side drop

Green strip

Foot drop

(c)
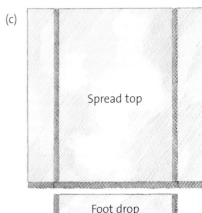
Spread top

Foot drop

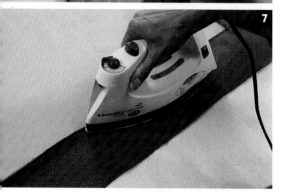

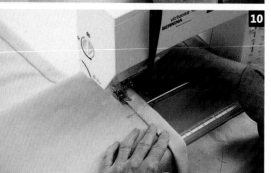

6 Right sides together and raw edges aligned, pin and stitch a green side strip (4 by 83½ inches) to a side edge of the spread top. Finish the seam allowances.

7 With the piece wrong side up, press the seam allowances toward the spread top.

8 With the right side up, topstitch ⅜ inch from the seam on the spread top, stitching through all thicknesses. Repeat to attach a side strip to the other edge of the spread top.

9 Right sides together and raw edges aligned, pin and stitch the green foot strip (4 by 55 inches) to the foot of the spread top, including the green side strips. Finish the seam allowances, press them toward the spread top, and topstitch as you did the sides.

10 To make the hems on each drop, turn up 2 inches, wrong sides together, and press. Turn the raw edge in to meet the pressed fold; pin and stitch.

11 To make a trim piece for a drop, pin two short green strips, right sides together, along one long side and one end; stitch the pinned edges. Turn right side out and press. Repeat to join three more pairs of green strips.

12 Lay the left drop on your work surface, right side up, with the hem toward you. At the *right* edge of the drop, align the raw edges of a green trim piece made in the previous step, as shown; pin and stitch.

13 Finish the seam allowances, press them toward the drop, and topstitch.

14 Repeat with the right side drop and another green trim piece, adding the trim piece to the *left* end of the drop.

15 Right sides together and long raw edges aligned, sew each side drop to the spread top, making sure the drops' green trim pieces are at the foot (not the head) of the spread. (You'll have an extra ½ inch of the green foot strip showing underneath because that edge is

not yet finished, while the end of each side drop *is* finished.) Finish the seam allowances, press them toward the drops, and topstitch.

16 Add green trim pieces to each end of the foot drop as you did for the sides.

17 With right sides together and raw edges aligned, pin and stitch the foot drop to the spread top. Finish the seam allowances, press them toward the drop, and topstitch. The side drops and the foot drop are now attached to the spread top.

Attaching the Tongues

18 Finish the long raw edges and one short raw edge on each tongue piece. Hem the remaining edge as you hemmed the drops (see Step 10).

19 Fold each piece in half lengthwise. On the unhemmed edge, clip *a scant ½ inch* into the fabric to mark the midpoint.

20 With the *right* side of a tongue piece against the *wrong* sides of the drops in one corner, pin the unhemmed edge of the tongue to the tops of the drops, opening the clip and aligning it with the corner. Stitch, pivoting carefully at the clip. Repeat with another tongue piece on the other corner.

21 At the head of the spread, turn under 6 inches and press. Turn the raw edge in to meet the pressed fold; pin and stitch to make the hem.

Adding the Grommets

22 Working on the right side of the foot and side drops, measure and mark four equidistant points on the length of each green trim piece, 1½ inches from the outer edge.

23 For each trim piece, place a block of wood underneath the fabric. Position the grommet cutter over each mark and hit firmly with a hammer.

24 Set the grommets.

25 Clip the top two pairs of grommets together on each corner with the carabiners.

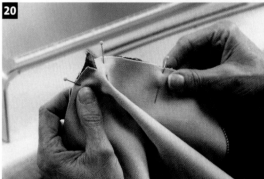

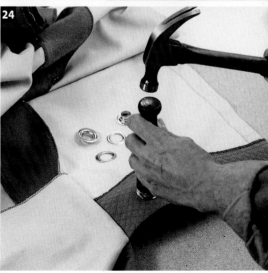

Innovative
Elements

Platform Chair
An inflatable chair sits on a plywood platform screwed to four unused quart-size paint cans (available at home centers and paint stores). Multicolored rope lights on the plywood edge were tacked in place with a staple gun.

Funnel Lamp

BELOW: This one-of-a-kind lamp, with a real funnel for its shade, is perfect for reading in bed. You can buy the funnel and gooseneck tubing at home centers; check out lighting stores for the inner workings.

Saucer Lights

ABOVE: A contemporary cable light system with adjustable saucer-shaped spotlights accentuates the sweeping ceiling line and draws the eye upward.

Window Headings
Words painted above the windows encourage this child to reach for the stars. Print the words or letters using a computer's printer, then enlarge them at a photocopy shop to make a pattern. Use graphite paper to transfer the pattern to the wall.

DISCOVER

Rustic Quarters

OUTFITTED WITH A CACTUS HAT TREE, a comfy flannel throw, and a valance made of real corrugated metal, this room is a perfect outpost for a young boy to sleep, sprawl, roughhouse, read, and daydream. A storage unit composed of stacked cubes holds books, toys, and other gear; a play surface coated with blackboard paint and mounted on casters pulls out from under the bed, providing another spot for creative pursuits. Graphic stenciled motifs continue the rugged theme and add visual punch to walls that were left their original color. Patterns for the motifs are on pages 112 through 114.

Khaki-colored walls, a large casement window, and an old painted bed frame made great starting points for the reinvention of this space.

MATERIALS

4- by 8-foot sheet of
¾-inch MDF

Flexible electrical cord

Felt-tip marker

Eye and ear protection

Jigsaw

Electric drill

⅝-inch Forstner bit

Paint roller, paint tray,
and liner

Paintbrush

Latex primer

Green, red, blue, and
purple latex paint

Electric sander

Lime green paint marker

Miter box or hacksaw

12 feet of ⅝-inch
doweling

Wood glue

Plastic cup

Cotton swabs

Circular saw

Five 1¼-inch wood
screws

FINISHED SIZE

45 by 95 inches

IN A WEEKEND

Cactus Hat Tree

A CARTOON-STYLE CACTUS made of medium-density fiberboard (MDF) provides this boy with a place to hang his hat—as well as other important belongings. A wide base keeps the tall unit stable. Green latex paint and a paint marker color the cactus. Red, blue, and purple pegs at crazy angles serve as make-believe spines.

TIP

YOU DON'T NEED A DEGREE
IN ART TO CREATE YOUR
OWN CACTUS—THE SECRET
DESIGN TOOL IS A FLEXIBLE
CORD (SEE STEP 1). IF YOU'RE
RELUCTANT TO DRAW DIRECTLY
ON THE MDF, LOCATE A
BLUEPRINT SERVICE THAT
WILL SELL YOU LARGE SHEETS
OF PLAIN PAPER. TAPE THE
SHEETS TOGETHER AND
MAKE A PATTERN, THEN USE
THE PATTERN TO DRAW THE
CACTUS OUTLINE ON THE MDF.

Cutting Out the Cactus

1 Draw the cactus trunk freehand on the MDF, making the bottom approximately 14 inches wide and tapering the trunk slightly as you go up, using wavy rather than straight lines. Lay out the electrical cord to shape the rest of the cactus. Outline the shape with a pencil; go over the pencil lines with the marker.

2 Wearing eye and ear protection, cut out the cactus with the jigsaw.

3 At the base of the cactus, measure and mark a centered, 3-inch-deep notch that's ¾ inch wide (as wide as the MDF is thick). Cut out the notch with the jigsaw.

4 Using the electric drill and ⅝-inch Forstner bit, drill holes randomly for the pegs on the upper trunk and the arms of the cactus, stopping at the base of the bit. (Drill a test hole on a scrap of MDF first to make sure the bit doesn't go all the way through.)

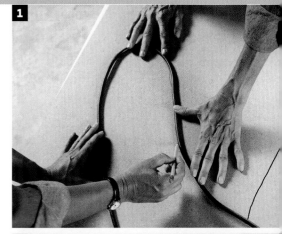

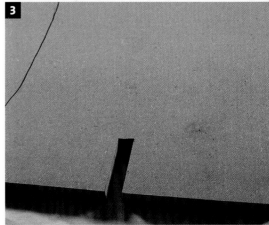

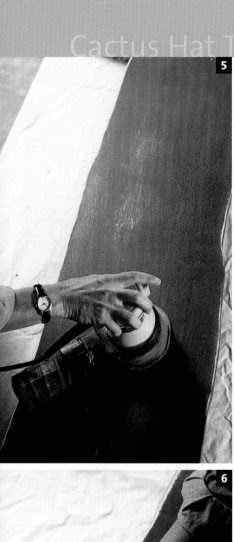

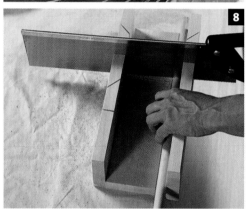

Painting the Cactus

5 Prime the front, back, and edges of the cactus, then paint the surfaces green. In scattered places, sand the surface with the electric sander just to the point where the primer shows.

6 Using the lime green paint marker, outline the perimeter of the cactus. Add interior lines for the ribs. (Note in the photo on page 98 that the lines split off from the trunk at the branches.)

7 Sand the lines to soften them until they resemble chalk lines. Sand parts of the cactus's outer edges down to the MDF to give the surface a slightly weathered look.

Adding the Dowels

8 Using the miter box or hacksaw, cut pegs 3 to 5 inches long from the doweling.

9 Paint the pegs red, blue, and purple; allow them to dry.

10 Pour wood glue into a plastic cup. Dip one end of a peg into the glue, then use a cotton swab to lightly coat the hole with glue. Push the peg into the hole, wiping away any excess glue with a clean swab. Repeat with the remaining pegs, varying the angles of placement. Allow to dry.

19 On the remaining short piece, bind the lower edge as in Steps 10 and 11.

20 With raw edges aligned and right sides facing up, place the short piece on top of the long piece and the lining. Pin the raw edges from clip to clip.

21 Turn the pieces over (the lining will be faceup) and carefully remove the pins, keeping the edges aligned. As you did on the footboard slipcover, pin and stitch the binding to the remaining edges, beginning and ending at the clips. Bring the binding to the front and topstitch close to the fold.

22 Hand-sew a double tie at the midpoint on each side of the headboard slipcover.

23 To make the skirt, pin the skirt quilt piece to the skirt lining piece with right sides together and raw edges aligned. Stitch, leaving an 8-inch opening along one long edge. Trim the corners to reduce bulk, turn right side out, and slipstitch the opening closed.

24 Hand-sew a double tie on each top corner of the skirt and at the ladder.

25 Slip the pieces over the foot and head of the bed and tie the double ties. Tie the skirt to the foot.

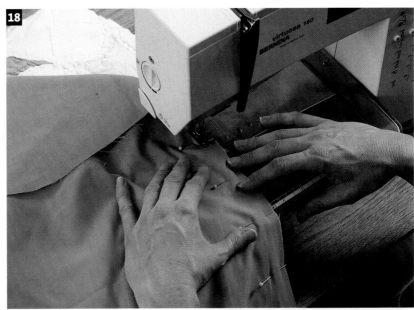

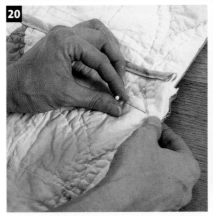

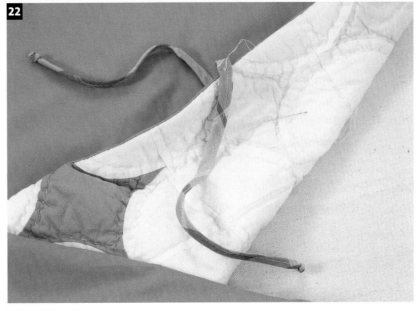

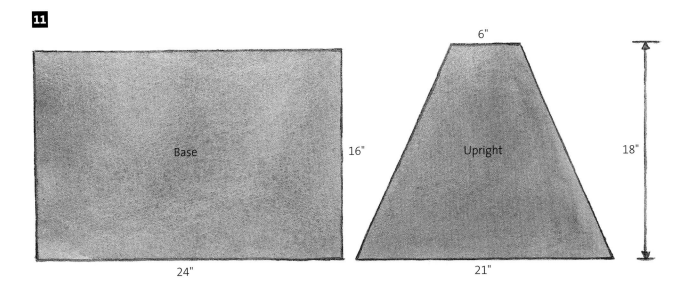

Base   16"   24"

6"   Upright   18"   21"

Making the Support Unit

11 Measure and mark the base and upright pieces for the support unit from MDF. The dimensions of the support pieces for this cactus are shown above. Cut out with the circular saw.

12 Starting at the upper edge of the upright piece, cut a centered, ¾-inch-wide notch, stopping 3 inches from the lower edge. (The short notch in the cactus, cut in Step 3, will slip into this long notch.)

13 Prime and paint one side of the base and all edges green. (One side is left unpainted for easy marking.) Prime and paint the upright piece on both sides and all edges. Allow to dry.

14 Center the upright piece on the unpainted side of the base and draw an outline around it. Predrill

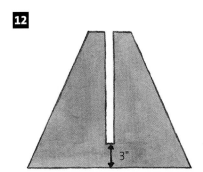

3"

five evenly spaced holes in the base within the outline. Turn the base over; carefully center and outline the upright on the painted side.

15 With a helper, place the upright piece upside down, under and against the painted side of the base so that it's positioned precisely within the outline. Screw the base to the upright piece.

Assembling the Hat Tree

16 Turn the support unit right side up and slide the cactus into the upright piece.

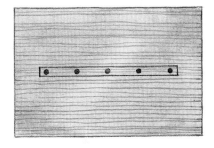

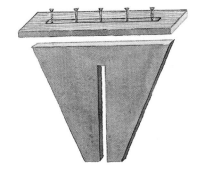

MATERIALS

Masking tape

4- by 14-inch rotary ruler

⅝ yard *each* of 16 different all-cotton flannel fabrics, 42 inches wide

22- by 34-inch rotary cutting mat

Rotary cutter

6- by 24-inch rotary ruler

Fabric marker

1⅝ yards of 80/20 quilt batting, 90 inches wide

Walking foot*

All-cotton thread

Fabric scissors

*Read the introduction on page 10.

NOTE: Do not prewash fabrics.

SEWING WORKSHOP

Frayed Flannel Throw

THIS SOFT FLANNEL THROW with seam allowances on the outside is reminiscent of early doll blankets. To make the squares, you sandwich a piece of batting between two pieces of flannel, then anchor the layers with stitching. After the squares are joined, you clip the exposed seam allowances and wash and dry the throw. The result? A comfy, cuddly blanket that's an instant favorite.

FINISHED SIZE

56 by 72 inches

TIP

COTTON FLANNEL IS EITHER

WOVEN OR PRINTED. WOVEN

FLANNEL—WHICH LOOKS THE

SAME ON BOTH SIDES—IS

IDEAL FOR THIS KIND OF

PROJECT BECAUSE ITS

EXPOSED SEAM ALLOWANCES

WILL BE THE SAME COLOR

AS THE SQUARES. WITH

PRINTED FLANNEL, THE SEAM

ALLOWANCES WILL PROBABLY

BE LIGHTER. (THIS THROW

INCLUDES BOTH KINDS OF

FLANNEL.)

Making the Squares

1 This project uses 1-inch seam allowances. To make a seam guide, layer several pieces of masking tape so their edges are precisely aligned. Position the 4- by 14-inch rotary ruler under the needle at the 1-inch mark; place the layered tape so it just touches the right-hand edge of the ruler. Use the edge of the layered tape as a guide when you stitch the seams.

2 Lay a ⅝-yard piece of flannel, folded in half as it was on the bolt, on your cutting mat so it extends just beyond the marked lines of a 20-inch square. (Look carefully at the lines and count the 1-inch squares to make sure the flannel overlaps a 20-inch area.) Using your rotary cutter and 6- by 24-inch ruler, trim the edges, including the folded edge, to make a 20-inch square. Cut the square in half at 10 inches across.

3 Turn the cutting mat (not the fabric) and cut a perpendicular line through the layered flannel, again at 10 inches across.

4 You'll now have four 10-inch squares, each consisting of a double layer of flannel.

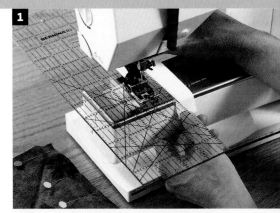

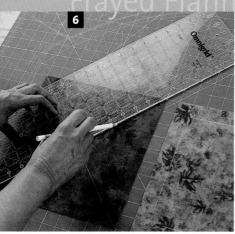

5 Pin each flannel pair together. Cut the remaining ⁵/₈-yard pieces of flannel to make a total of 64 pairs of squares; you'll use 63 pairs.

6 Unpin one pair of squares. On the right side of one square, use the fabric marker to draw a line diagonally from corner to corner in both directions. On the wrong side of the other square, draw guidelines for batting placement 1 inch from the cut edges.

7 Cut the batting into 63 squares, each 7³/₄ by 7³/₄ inches. (You cut the batting smaller than the fabric so it does not get caught in the seams when you join the flannel squares.)

8 Center a square of batting on the side of the flannel square marked with the placement guidelines. Keep in mind that the batting will be about ¹/₈ inch smaller all around than the marked square.

9 Place the other flannel square on top of the batting, right side up,

aligning the raw edges of the two squares. Pin along the diagonal lines through all layers, placing the pins perpendicular to the lines as shown. Also place one pin on each edge of the squares, parallel to the cut edges and through both layers, to keep them from shifting as you stitch.

10 Attach the walking foot to your sewing machine. Sew on one diagonal line, removing pins just before you reach them. Sew on the other line in the same way. Repeat to stitch the remaining flannel squares.

Joining the Squares

11 Lay out the squares on the floor with seven squares across and nine squares down. Label the squares in the first row by pinning slips of paper on them marked with the row number and square number; for example, "Row 1/Square 1." Label the squares in the remaining rows in the same way.

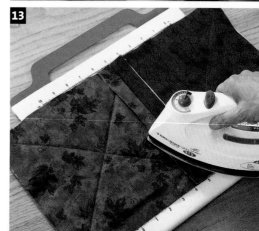

104

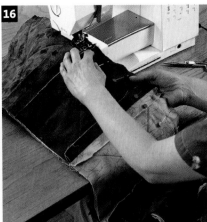

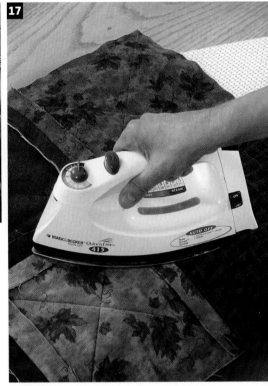

12 With the back sides together, pin the first two squares in Row 1 along one edge. Stitch.

13 Press the seam allowances open. This now becomes the "right side" of the throw, the side that will be frayed.

14 Join the remaining squares to make Row 1, always stitching with the seam allowances on the same side. Press the seam allowances open as you go.

15 Join the squares to make the remaining rows. Lay out the rows, in order, on the floor.

16 With the back sides together, pin the first two rows, matching the seams carefully. (Make sure the seam allowances on both rows will be on the front.) Stitch.

17 Press the seam allowances on the rows open.

18 Join and press the remaining rows. Stitch 1 inch from the outer edges of the throw.

Finishing the Throw

19 Carefully clip the seam allowances up to the seams every ³/₈ to ¹/₂ inch to create fringe. Be careful not to cut through the stitching, or you'll have holes in your throw. First clip the horizontal seams joining the rows; where seams meet, undo the stitching in the seam allowances. Then clip the vertical seam allowances; where they lie underneath the horizontal seam allowances, reach under and carefully clip the vertical seam allowances as close to the row stitching as possible. Finally, clip the outer edges.

20 Wash your throw in warm water on the regular cycle. Dry on medium heat, stopping the dryer every 10 minutes to remove lint from the lint trap. This step is essential because the clipped seam allowances create a great deal of lint, which can be a fire hazard when the dryer is operating.

21 Pick the lint and stray threads from the throw.

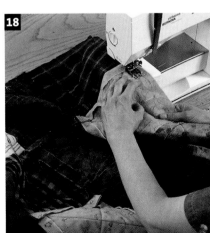

Metal Valance

AN INNOVATIVE WINDOW TREATMENT made of corrugated metal attached to a pine frame sets the scene and adds architectural interest to the room. Don't plan to cut the corrugated metal yourself; it requires special tools and protective gear. Ask a sheet-metal shop to cut the pieces and—very important—to smooth the sharp edges. Washing the metal with muriatic acid and rubbing it with an antiquing solution give it that authentic rusted look. Enlist the aid of a helper for this project.

FINISHED SIZE 18 inches tall, 60 inches wide, 10½ inches deep at the base

MATERIALS

6- by 24-inch rotary ruler, available at fabric stores and quilt shops

Pine 1 by 12, equal in length to the window width plus 2 feet*

Circular saw

Red latex paint

Paper towels

Electric drill with drill bits

Twelve 1¼-inch wood screws

Fan

Plastic drop cloth

Respirator

Heavy-duty rubber
or latex gloves

1 quart of muriatic acid,
available at home
centers and hardware
stores (read the label
warning carefully)

Disposable paint tray

Natural (sea) sponges

One 2- by 6-foot sheet
of corrugated metal,
cut into three 21½-inch
lengths**

Rust antiquing solution,
available at craft stores

Steel tape measure

Socket attachment
to the drill,
with socket driver

Eight hex-head
roofing screws

Stud finder

Carpenter's level

2½-inch wood screws
for mounting the
valance to studs

*For a window 54 inches
wide, the lumber must
be at least 6½ feet long.
See the tip on page 108.*

**For a window any wider
than 54 inches you'll
need two sheets of metal.*

Making the Pine Frame

1 For the frame's angled side pieces, use the rotary ruler to draw two triangles on the pine 1 by 12, each 18 inches high and the width of the board, as shown. Mark lines across the tips of the triangles where they measure ¾ inch wide; minus the tips, the sloping sides should measure approximately 19¾ inches.

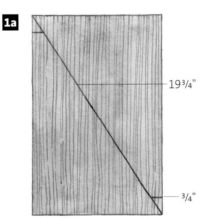

19¾"

¾"

2 Cut the marked pieces using the circular saw. Measure, mark, and cut three 1- by 4-inch pine pieces, each as long as the window width plus 6 inches, minus the actual thickness of the side pieces. (Most 1-by lumber is approximately ¾ inch thick.) These slats will fit between the angled side pieces and support the valance from the back.

3 Paint the sides and slats red using paper towels. Strive for a streaked, color-washed effect. Allow the paint to dry.

4 With the aid of a helper, position the upper slat between the side pieces 1 inch down from the top, aligning the back edges of the slat and the sides. Using the electric drill and 1¼-inch wood screws, attach the sides to the upper slat, placing two screws at each end. Attach the bottom slat to the inside front of the side pieces, following the angle. Attach the middle slat in the same way.

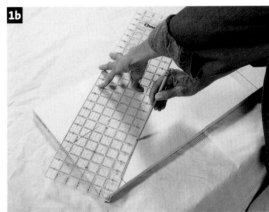

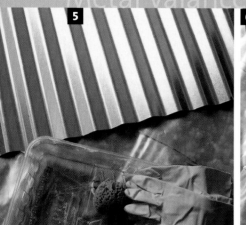

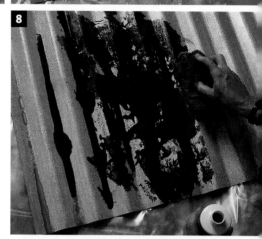

"Rusting" the Metal

5 Take the following precautions: Work outdoors near a faucet. Set up the fan to blow the fumes away from you. Protect the ground with a plastic drop cloth. Wear a respirator and heavy-duty gloves.

6 Pour a small amount of the muriatic acid into the disposable paint tray. Using a slightly damp sponge, wipe the muriatic acid onto the face of the metal sheets in a light scrubbing motion.

7 Allow the acid to remain on the metal for a few seconds. Wash off the acid with a spray attachment on a hose. (Water neutralizes the acid.) Dispose of the excess acid and the sponge and tray as directed on the acid label.

8 Using another sponge, apply three coats of the rust antiquing solution to the metal sheets according to the manufacturer's instructions; wipe off with clean rags.

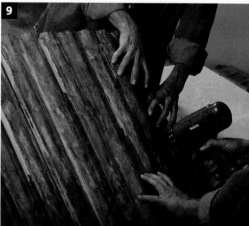

Predrilling the Metal

9 Lay the first sheet of metal on the right end of the frame so it overlaps the side by about 1½ inches and the top edge does not extend beyond the back of the upper slat. (If the metal sheet is attached too far up, it will hit the wall and you won't be able to mount the treatment.) Along the right edge of the metal, measure from the bottom-right corner to the midpoint of the lower slat. A few inches in from the end, at a "valley" in the corrugation, predrill a hole through the metal and into the lower slat. Predrill another hole through the metal and into the middle slat.

10 Measure the right end from the lower edge of the sheet positioned in the previous step to the *bottom* of the lower slat. You'll use this measurement to align the lower edges of the metal sheets.

11 Position a second piece of metal at the left end of the frame, using the measurement from the previous step. Predrill holes through the metal and into the lower and middle slats.

12 Position the third piece of metal in the middle, overlapping the pieces at the ends. Predrill holes through the metal and into the lower and middle slats.

Attaching the Metal Panels

13 Attach the metal to the wood frame using the socket attachment with socket driver and the hex-head roofing screws. Work in the same order—right piece, left piece, then middle piece. Unscrew the metal pieces from the frame and make adjustments, if necessary. Take the pieces off and label them. (You'll later mount the bare frame, then reattach the metal pieces.)

Mounting the Valance

14 Use the stud finder to locate the studs above the window; lightly mark the positions on the wall.

15 With a helper, hold up the frame at the desired height; mark the wall at several places across the width of the frame. Using a level, draw a horizontal line at the marks. Above the line, also lightly mark the studs so you'll know where to put in the screws.

16 Using the 2½-inch wood screws, attach the valance frame to the wall at the studs, through the upper slat.

17 Using the roofing screws, reattach the metal sheets to the wood frame.

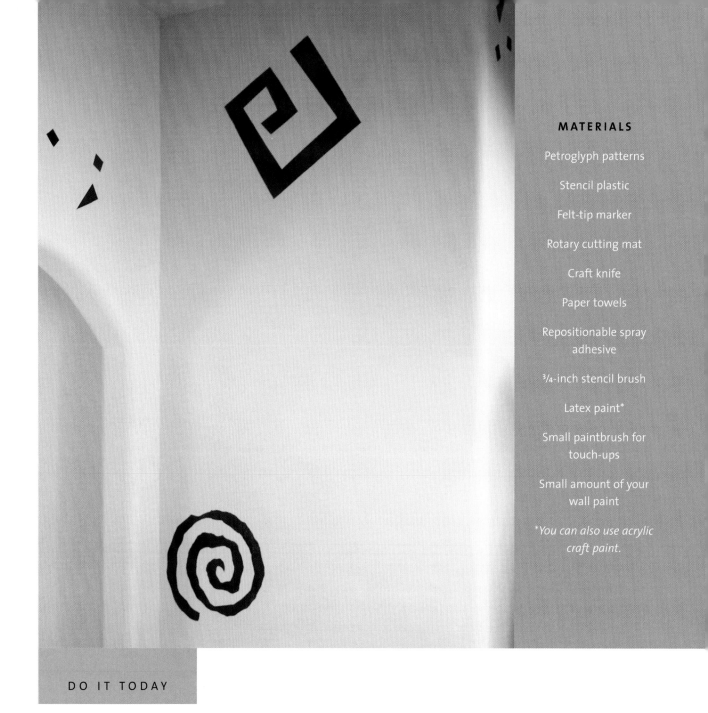

MATERIALS

Petroglyph patterns

Stencil plastic

Felt-tip marker

Rotary cutting mat

Craft knife

Paper towels

Repositionable spray
adhesive

¾-inch stencil brush

Latex paint*

Small paintbrush for
touch-ups

Small amount of your
wall paint

*You can also use acrylic
craft paint.

DO IT TODAY

Petroglyph Walls

ABSTRACT MOTIFS add a splash of color to neutral walls and bring to mind primitive rock drawings. Enlarge the shapes shown here using the patterns provided on the following pages or draw your own. If you opt to create original designs, keep them simple and chunky for maximum impact. Latex paint has a tendency to seep under stencils, so plan to touch up the edges of the motifs with a small paintbrush.

TIP

FOR BEST RESULTS, USE

LESS RATHER THAN MORE

PAINT; YOU CAN ALWAYS

GO OVER AREAS THAT

NEED MORE COLOR, BUT

YOU CAN'T REMOVE PAINT.

110

Step by Step

Making the Stencil

1 Enlarge the patterns to the indicated dimensions at a photocopy shop. Lay stencil plastic over each motif and trace the lines with the felt-tip marker.

2 Working on the rotary cutting mat, cut along the lines with the craft knife.

Stenciling the Motifs

3 Cover your work surface with paper towels. Spray the back of a stencil with repositionable adhesive.

4 Position the stencil on the wall and press firmly to adhere. Dip the stencil brush into the paint, then dab the brush on paper towels to remove the excess.

5 Holding the stencil brush perpendicular to the wall, pounce (dab) the paint onto the wall through the cutout area of the stencil. Be careful not to push the paint under the edge of the stencil.

6 Remove the stencil and allow the paint to dry.

7 Repeat Steps 3 through 6 to stencil the other motifs on the wall. Touch up the edges, if needed, with the small paintbrush and a little of your wall paint.

15¼"

11¾"

Petroglyph patterns. See Step 1 on page 111.

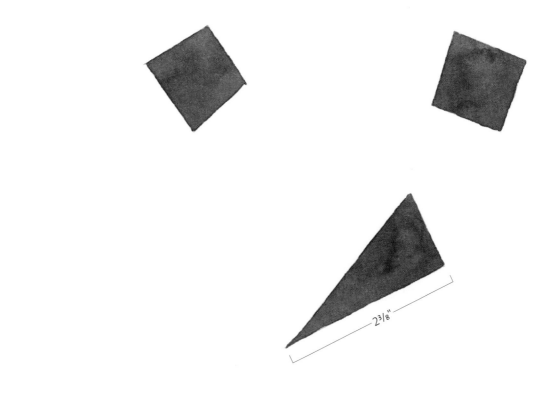

2³⁄₈"

12¹⁄₄"

10"

11"

Petroglyph patterns. See Step 1 on page 111.

Roll-away Play Surface

WHAT CHILD COULDN'T USE more floor space in his or her room? This under-the-bed surface on casters pulls out for an extra play station and rolls away when it's time to pick up. Blackboard paint provides a budding artist with a floor-level drawing surface. You can cut the pieces of MDF yourself or have them cut at a home center, lumberyard, or cabinet shop.

FINISHED SIZE 31 inches wide, 41 inches long, 4¾ inches tall

TIP

IF YOU HAVE THE MDF PIECES CUT, BE SURE TO ASK FOR THE SCRAPS; THEY'RE HELPFUL WHEN YOU BEGIN TO ATTACH THE SIDE PIECES TO THE BLACKBOARD SURFACE.

MATERIALS

Steel tape measure

4 by 4 feet (a half-sheet) of ¾-inch MDF

4 by 4 feet (a half-sheet) of ½-inch MDF

Circular saw

Latex primer

Paintbrush

120-grit sandpaper

Blackboard paint

Carpenter's square

Adjustable miter box with backsaw

Router with roundover bit or 60-grit sandpaper

Red latex paint

Wood glue

Hammer

Ten ¾-inch finishing nails

Electric drill

Fourteen ¾-inch screws

Wood putty or spackle

Four ⅝-inch corner brackets with screws

Two drawer pulls with screws

Four 2½-inch casters with screws

Cutting the Pieces

1 Measure and mark a 30- by 40-inch rectangle on the ¾-inch MDF. Cut the piece with the circular saw. Save the scraps.

2 On the ½-inch MDF, measure and mark four strips, each 3¼ inches wide by the length of the half-sheet. Cut the strips with the circular saw. Save the scraps.

Painting the Blackboard Surface

3 Prime one side of the 30- by 40-inch MDF piece; sand lightly with 120-grit sandpaper. Paint the primed side with the blackboard paint, following the manufacturer's instructions.

Attaching the Sides

4 Using the carpenter's square, measure and mark a line 1⅝ inches from the edge along the length of each side piece. You'll use this line as a guide to attach the sides in Step 9.

5 On your work surface, lay scraps of ¾- and ½-inch MDF on top of each other to make a platform that's 1¼ inches tall. Lay the blackboard surface, painted side up, on the MDF platform.

TIP

IF THE VERTICAL CLEARANCE UNDER YOUR CHILD'S BED IS LESS THAN 5 INCHES, YOU'LL NEED TO MAKE THE SIDE PIECES NARROWER (THESE ARE 3¼ INCHES) OR BUY SHORTER, SMALLER CASTERS— OR BOTH.

6 Working with one side piece at a time, miter the corners using the adjustable miter box. It's easiest and most accurate to make a 45-degree-angle cut on one end of a side piece, hold the piece against the blackboard surface, mark the spot on the other end for the second angled cut, then make the second cut.

7 Use the router with roundover bit or use 60-grit sandpaper to round the upper edge of each piece.

8 Prime, sand with the 120-grit sandpaper, and paint the unmarked face of each side piece red. (Do not paint the mitered cuts.) Allow the paint to dry; apply a second coat.

9 Apply wood glue to each mitered cut. Set each side piece on its edge with the painted face against the blackboard surface. Using the hammer and finishing nails, attach each side piece to the blackboard surface, nailing at the marked line. Use three nails on each long side, placing one in the middle and one 3 inches from each end; use two nails on each short side, placing one 3 inches from each end.

10 Predrill equidistant holes for the ¾-inch screws on each side piece along the marked line, spacing them outside and between the nails, four on each long side and three on each short side.

11 Screw the sides to the blackboard surface.

12 Fill the holes and mitered corners with wood putty or spackle; sand with 120-grit sandpaper. Prime and paint the upper edges and outer surfaces of the side pieces red. Allow the paint to dry; sand lightly and apply a second coat.

Attaching the Hardware

13 Mark the screw holes for the corner brackets. Also mark screw holes for the drawer pulls on the shorter side pieces.

14 Predrill the holes for the corner brackets and attach them.

15 Predrill the holes for the drawer pulls and attach them.

16 Attach the casters to the underside of the play surface at the corners.

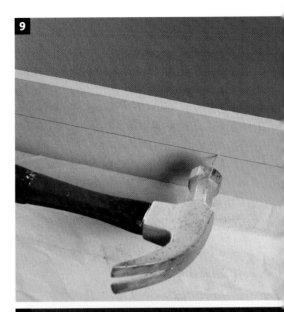

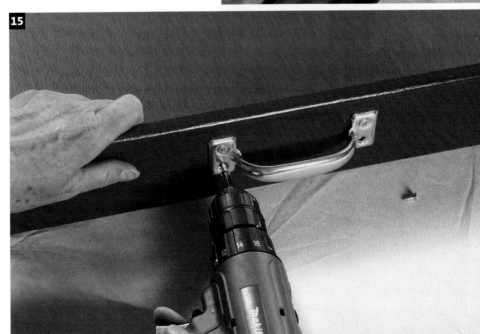

MATERIALS

Lid or plate for marking curved corners

¾-inch MDF, 33 by 13¾ inches, for the bottom platform*

½-inch MDF, 33 by 13¾ inches, for the middle platform*

Jigsaw

Router with a roundover bit or 60-grit sandpaper

Four storage cubes*
• Lower (two cubes): 12 by 12 by 32 inches
• Middle: 24 by 12 by 16 inches
• Upper: 12 by 12 by 12 inches

100-grit sandpaper

Trisodium phosphate, available at home centers and hardware stores

IN A WEEKEND

Storage Tower

A MODULAR STORAGE UNIT helps clear out the clutter that accumulates in a child's room. Inexpensive storage cubes come in all sizes; most have a tough finish that you'll need to sand and prime in preparation for painting. This tower unit was configured with a space between the lower cubes to accommodate oversize books and sketch pads. Exposed hardware—T-hinges and simple hooks—give the unit its rugged look. Whether or not your child tends to climb, attach the tower to the wall for safety.

FINISHED SIZE

32½ inches wide,

13¾ inches deep,

64¾ inches tall

Step by Step

Preparing the Pieces

1 Using the lid or plate, mark curves for the two front corners of each MDF platform.

2 Cut the curves with the jigsaw.

3 Using the router with a round-over bit or using 60-grit sandpaper, round the front and side edges of each MDF platform.

4 Assemble the cubes following the manufacturer's instructions. Sand the cubes with 100-grit sand-paper. Wash them with trisodium phosphate.

Painting the Pieces

5 Prime the outer surfaces and edges of the cubes with the bonding primer, and paint with the latex paint. Prime, sand, and paint both sides and the edges of the plat-forms. In this storage tower, the lower cubes and bottom platform are red, the middle cubes and middle platform are green, and the upper cube is blue. Apply two more coats of paint to each piece.

Assembling the Tower

NOTE: In the following steps, the colors of the components are provided in parentheses. Refer to the illustration on page 120 for Steps 7 through 10.

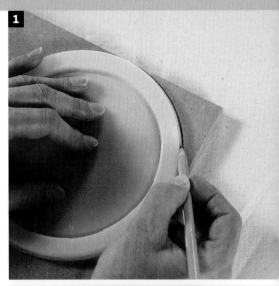

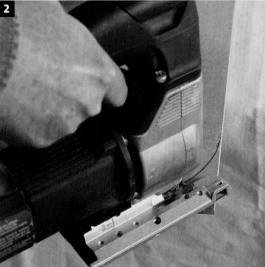

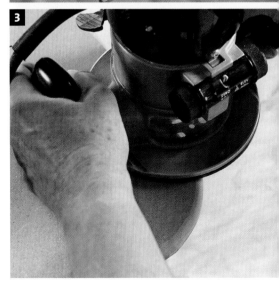

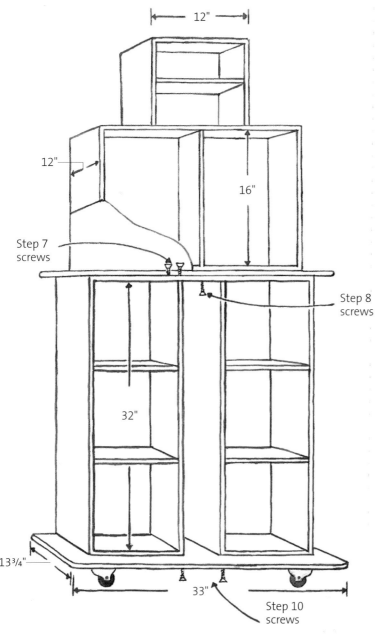

12"

12"

16"

Step 7
screws

Step 8
screws

32"

13¾"

33"

Step 10
screws

The illustration above shows the placement and direction of the screws.

7 Clamp the middle (green) platform to the lower (red) cubes, protecting the platform surface with waxed paper if necessary. Using the combination countersink–pilot hole drill bit, predrill two holes through the platform and into each cube, placing one hole 2 inches from the back edge and the other 2 inches from the front edge. Screw the platform to the cubes using ¾-inch screws; countersink the screws. See photo 7 and the illustration at left.

8 Turn the unit upside down and center it on top of the middle (green) cube, with the back edges aligned. Predrill two holes through the middle platform and into the vertical center piece of the middle cube, placing one hole near the front and one hole near the back of the cube. Screw the platform to the cube using 1-inch screws.

6 Stand the lower (red) cubes on your work surface or on the floor, side by side, with 5 inches (or the distance you planned for) between them. Place the middle (green) platform on top of the cubes, with the back edges aligned. On the long edges of the platform, measure and mark the midpoint using the carpenter's square and the awl. Also mark points 2½ inches (or half the distance between the cubes) on either side of the midpoint.

9 Attach the casters to one side of the bottom (red) platform, positioning them near the corners.

10 With the unit still upside down, position the bottom platform (with the casters up) on the lower (red) cubes, keeping the back edges of the cubes and the platform flush. Standing on a stepladder, predrill two holes through the platform and into each cube's inner vertical edge, placing one hole at the front and one hole at the back; attach with 1-inch screws. (The outer edges of the cubes will be secured to the platform with hinges.)

11 Turn the unit right side up. Attach the 4-inch hinges to the outside edges of each lower (red) cube and the bottom platform. Attach the 3-inch hinges to the outside edges of the middle (green) cube and the middle platform.

12 Center the upper (blue) cube on top of the middle cube, with the back edges flush. Attach a 3-inch hinge to each side of the upper cube and the top of the middle cube.

13 Attach a robe hook to each lower (red) cube.

14 Locate a stud in the wall. Attach the L-bracket to the underside of the middle (green) cube, centered in the gap, and attach the tower to the wall at the stud.

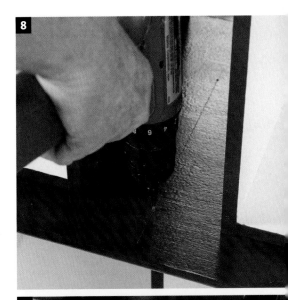

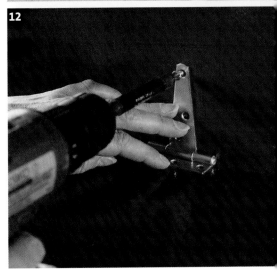

Parfait Dreams

LIKE LAYERS ON AN ICE-CREAM CAKE, bands of pastel color encircle this little girl's room, setting the scene for a collection of sweet furnishings and accessories. Patterned fabric for the box-pleated valance suggested the pretty color palette. An oversize ottoman fashioned from rounds of foam and covered in a bright pink check plays off the wall stripes, while the painted peg rail blends right in. A trio of bookcases, transformed from unfinished wood furniture into life-size dollhouses, adds charm and child-friendly "architectural interest."

A small space with a single window, this room offered no special features to inspire its transformation.

MATERIALS

Steel tape measure

Cotton fabric,
54 or 60 inches wide*

Lining, 48 inches
wide or wider*

Carpenter's square

6- by 24-inch rotary
ruler, available at fabric
stores and quilt shops

Fabric scissors

Pins

Thread to blend

Bib overalls, one for each
foot of window width

Wood curtain rod
and brackets

Double-sided tape
or pushpins

*See Steps 1 and 2
for yardage.

NOTE: Do not prewash
fabrics. Plan to
dry-clean the valance
when needed.

DO IT TODAY

Bib-top Valance

BIB OVERALLS ADD A TOUCH OF WHIMSY to a box-pleated valance. Box pleats look casual but require a bit of patience and some simple math. As a rule of thumb, plan to have one box pleat, with bib heading, for every foot of window width. This window opening, for example, is 48 inches wide; the valance features four pleats. Look at thrift stores for secondhand overalls, which have a soft, lived-in look.

FINISHED SIZE 9½ inches long (not including bib tabs) by 54 inches wide

Calculating Yardage

1 Measure the width of the window opening. Add the side hems (2 inches each), two returns, two extensions, 12 inches for each box pleat, and 1 inch for good measure. (For an explanation of returns and extensions, see the tip at left.) Divide the total by the width of the fabric (typically 54 inches for home decorating fabrics, 48 inches for lining) to arrive at the number of fabric widths required; round up to the nearest whole number.

2 To arrive at the face fabric yardage, multiply the number of fabric widths by 18 inches. (If your fabric has a pattern, allow extra to match the pattern at the seams; ask a salesperson for help.) Divide by 36 for the yards needed. For the lining, multiply the number of fabric widths by 10 inches; divide by 36 for the yards needed. Add ¼ yard of each fabric for good measure.

Cutting and Joining the Widths

3 Using the carpenter's square and rotary ruler, square off and trim one cut end of the face fabric. From the squared-off end, measure down each selvage 14 inches; clip. Mark and cut across the fabric between the clips. Repeat to cut the remaining lengths. Trim the selvages. Set aside the leftover fabric for Step 12.

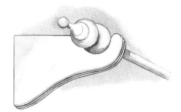

TIP

A "RETURN" IS THE DISTANCE THE TREATMENT WILL HANG FROM THE WALL, BASED ON THE BRACKET DEPTH. FOR EACH BRACKET IN THIS TREATMENT, THE RETURN IS 3½ INCHES. AN "EXTENSION" IS THE DISTANCE THE VALANCE EXTENDS ON EACH SIDE OF THE WINDOW OPENING. EACH EXTENSION FOR THIS TREATMENT IS 3 INCHES.

Mapping the Pleats

To hide the face fabric seams in the pleats in Step 5, add up the elements starting from the left as shown to see where the first seam will fall. If you're lucky, it will fall within a "pleat loop" and be hidden. If it will fall on the front of the valance, you'll need to trim the face fabric so the seam will fall in the pleat. (Always double-check your measurements before trimming face fabric.) Map out the entire valance to determine where to place the seams. It's not necessary to do the same with the lining because none of the lining seams will show on the front.

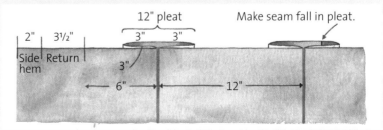

12" pleat — 3" — 3" — Make seam fall in pleat.
2" — 3½"
Side hem — Return — 3"
← 6" → — ← 12" →

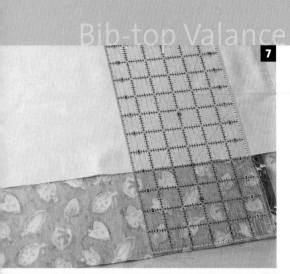

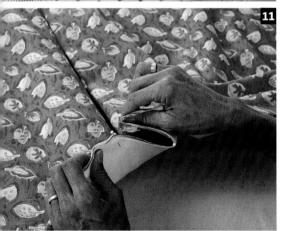

4 Repeat to measure and cut the lining fabric, making each piece 10 inches long.

5 To join fabric pieces so the seams will be hidden in the pleats, first make a pleat map (see the previous page). Based on your pleat map, trim the face fabric pieces, *making sure you include ½ inch for each seam allowance.*

6 With right sides together and raw edges aligned, pin the face fabric pieces, matching patterns if necessary. Using a ½-inch seam allowance, stitch the pieces to make one panel. Press the seams open. Repeat with the lining pieces.

Pinning the Pleats

7 Lay the face fabric panel on your work surface, wrong side up. Lay the lining panel, right side up, on the face fabric with the upper raw edges aligned and pinned. You should have 4 inches of the face fabric showing below the lining. Trim the lining panel 2 inches from each side of the face fabric panel.

8 Starting from one side, measure in 2 inches for the side hem, the number of inches for the return (3½ inches on this valance), and another 6 inches. Place a pin at that point on the upper edge to mark the start of the first box pleat.

9 From the pin, measure and pin four 3-inch increments on the upper edge for the first box pleat.

10 From the last pin in the pleat, measure and pin a 12-inch space. Measure and pin the second box pleat, followed by another 12-inch space. Measure and pin the remaining pleats, ending with a 6-inch space, a return (3½ inches on this valance), and a 2-inch side hem.

11 At each pleat, bring the first and fourth pins together to form a pleat loop. Flatten the pleat loop and pin; baste along the upper edge. Press the upper edge lightly.

Facing and Hemming the Valance

12 For the facing, cut two 4-inch strips across the width of the left-over face fabric; trim the selvages. Right sides together and raw edges aligned, join the short ends of the strips using a ½-inch seam allowance. Press the seam open. Trim the facing so it is equal in length to the width of the pleated panel, minus the side hems (see photo 13).

13 Stitch a narrow hem by machine on one long edge of the facing. With right sides together and upper raw edges aligned, pin the facing to the upper edge of the valance. Stitch using a ½-inch seam allowance. Press the seam

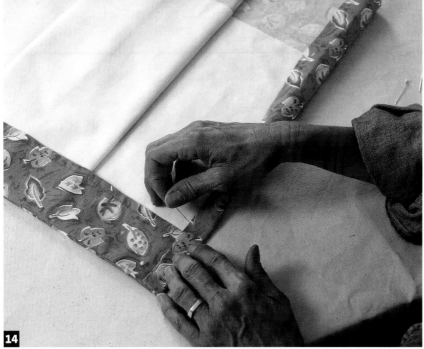

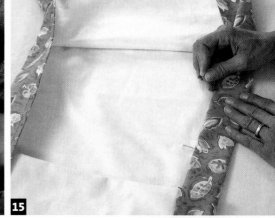

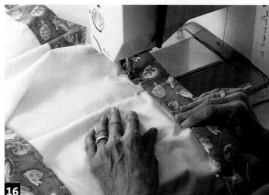

allowances and facing up, away from the valance, then press the seam allowances and facing down, toward the lining.

14 Fold each side hem of the face fabric in 2 inches and press the fold. Turn the raw edge in to meet the pressed fold; pin. Machine-stitch close to the inside fold.

15 At the lower edge of the valance, coax open the pleats so the panel lies flat. Fold up the hem 4 inches and press the fold. Turn the raw edge in to meet the pressed fold; pin.

16 Machine-stitch the hem close to the inside fold.

Adding the Bib Heading

17 Cut off the top part of the bibs on the overalls about ¹/₂ inch below the stitching, as shown. Cut off the straps in the back just above where they join, keeping the

maximum length. Wash and dry the pieces to fray the edges.

18 Unhook the straps. Center and pin each bib over a pleat so the top of the bib extends slightly above the top of the valance. Pin the corresponding straps to the facing on the back, centered behind the buttons, and hook the straps to each bib. Slip the rod through the straps and adjust them so the bibs hang just below the rod. Remove the rod. Topstitch across the top of each bib, stitching through all thicknesses. Trim the straps on the back 1 inch below the stitching.

Installing the Treatment

19 Mount the curtain hardware following the manufacturer's instructions. Slip the rod through the straps and set it in the brackets. Attach the ends of the valance to the insides of the brackets with tape or pushpins.

127

MATERIALS

Circular saw or handsaw

Miter box with backsaw

3½-inch colonial
base molding* for the
peg railing

1-by-4 plain molding*
for the shelf

1¼-inch lipped
molding* for the
shelf trim

Chalk line

Electric drill with a
drill bit the size of the
peg shank diameter

Wood glue

Pegs

Latex primer

Paintbrush

100-grit sandpaper

Latex paint

Stud finder

2-inch wood screws

Combination
countersink–pilot
hole drill bit

Paintable wood putty

Brad nailer
with 1¼-inch nails

*Lengths should total
the room's perimeter,
plus a few feet.

IN A WEEKEND

Peg Rail

A PEG RAIL positioned at the top of the green stripe is useful for hanging clothes and other belongings, high above little heads. It also adds visual interest and display area to this small room without gobbling up valuable floor space. This simple project was created with pegs and three kinds of molding, all readily available at home centers and lumberyards.

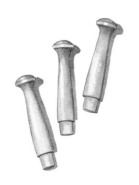

TIP

SELECT PEGS WHOSE SHANK
(THE NARROW PROJECTION AT
THE BACK) IS NO LONGER
THAN THE ACTUAL THICKNESS
OF THE BASE MOLDING.
OTHERWISE—IF, FOR EXAMPLE,
YOUR MOLDING MEASURES
½ INCH THICK AND THE PEG
SHANK MEASURES ⅝ INCH
LONG—THE SHANKS WILL
STICK OUT ON THE BACK.
CUTTING OFF THE SHANKS
AFTER THEY'RE INSERTED IS
DIFFICULT AND TEDIOUS.

Step by Step

1 Cut all the molding into lengths that correspond to each wall in the room, mitering the ends as needed. Determine the peg spacing you want and make it consistent from wall to wall (the pegs on this rail are 9 inches apart); leave space at the ends of each wall so you don't have pegs in the corners. It's best not to put the peg rail on a short wall or behind a door.

2 On the right side of the colonial base molding, snap a chalk line slightly above the midpoint. Mark the placement of the pegs on this line.

3 Place a scrap board underneath the base molding. Drill a hole for each peg, going all the way through the molding.

4 Put a little glue into each hole; insert the pegs. Let the glue dry.

5 To make the shelf, glue the lipped molding to one long edge of each piece of the plain molding. Also glue lipped molding to any exposed ends of plain molding at window or door openings. Let the glue dry.

6 Prime the rail and shelf pieces; sand lightly with the 100-grit sandpaper. Paint the pieces.

7 Attach the peg rail to the wall, placing the screws at the studs. Countersink the screws and fill with wood putty; sand. Touch up with the latex paint.

8 Position the shelf on top of the rail, with the back edge flush with the wall. Using the brad nailer and 1¼-inch nails, attach the shelf to the peg rail along the back edge every 12 inches.

Dollhouse Bookcase

SIDE-BY-SIDE BOOKCASES, complete with windows and doors, hold this little girl's collection of books, toys, and other treasured items. All three have scalloped roof slats and decorative brackets. The yellow-trimmed bookcase features shingles made from door skin (a thin veneer). Decorative molding trims the gable on the blue bookcase, while the gable on the pink bookcase is covered with siding made from the same molding as the roof slats. Materials and instructions for the yellow bookcase follow.

FINISHED SIZE yellow bookcase: 30 inches wide, 12 inches deep, 60 inches tall; blue bookcase: 72 inches tall; pink bookcase: 48 inches tall.

MATERIALS

Unfinished wood bookcase, 12 inches deep

Spiral saw

Latex primer

2-inch paintbrush

100-grit sandpaper

White latex paint

Wood clamps

Two 1-by-12 pine pieces, each equal in length to the bookcase width

Metal straightedge

Circular saw

One sheet of door skin, 36 by 84 inches

Circle template with 3- and 2¼-inch circles

30 feet of 2¼- by ⅜-inch pine molding

Electric brad nailer with ¾-inch nails

Two wood brackets

30 feet of ¾-inch corner guard trim*

Yellow latex paint

Four corner brackets with screws

Screwdriver

Adjustable miter box

Wood glue

TIP

TO CUT A WINDOW OPENING,

TIP THE SPIRAL SAW BLADE

INTO THE AREA TO BE CUT

OUT WITH THE SAW BLADE

RUNNING. WORK YOUR WAY

TOWARD A CORNER, THEN

CUT ON THE MARKED LINES.

Have an 18-inch section cut, then have one edge of the remaining trim "ripped" to 3/8 inch at the lumberyard or home center when you buy the pieces.

Preparing the Bookcase

1 The window openings on this bookcase are 3 by 5 inches; the doors are 5 by 12 inches. Measure, mark, and cut each window and door opening with the spiral saw.

2 Prime the bookcase; sand lightly with 100-grit sandpaper. Paint the bookcase with white latex paint.

Cutting the Gables and the Shingles

3 Clamp a 1-by-12 pine piece to your work surface. Measure and mark the midpoint along the upper edge. Mark a line from each lower corner to the upper midpoint, creating a triangle. Using the circular saw, cut on each line, beginning at the corner. Repeat to cut the second piece.

4 On the sheet of door skin, measure and mark three strips, each 3 inches wide by 84 inches long. Cut along the lines with the circular saw.

5 On each strip, mark pieces that are 5 inches long. Using the circle template, mark a 3-inch semicircle approximately 3/8 inch from one end on each piece.

6 Clamp a strip of the door skin to a scrap of wood. Cut the curve using the spiral saw, cutting through both the door skin and the scrap. (The scrap supports the strip and gives the saw more to cut into; see photo 6 on page 132.)

7 Unclamp the strip and shift it so the next marked curve is just beyond the newly cut curve in the scrap. (The curved scrap will support the strip on subsequent cuts.)

3

4

5
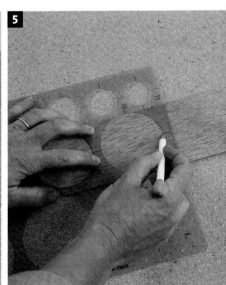

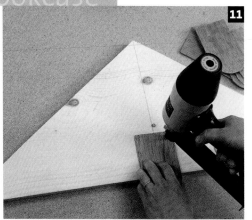

8 Cut the next curve, releasing the first shingle. Cut 38 shingles, plus a few extras.

9 Clamp a shingle to a scrap of wood with a straight edge, positioning it so the straight marked line on the shingle is just beyond the straight edge of the wood. Cut on the marked line, creating a shingle with one curved edge and one straight edge. Cut the remaining shingles in the same way.

Cutting the Roof Slats

10 On the 2¼-inch-wide pieces of molding, mark 14-inch-long strips for the roof slats (this bookcase required 18 slats). Mark a 2¼-inch semicircle on one end of each strip. Cut the curved lines with the spiral saw and the straight lines with the circular saw.

Attaching the Shingles

11 Lay one gable on your work surface. Mark a line from the peak to the midpoint on the lower edge. Center a shingle on the line, with the curve overlapping the gable (see the tip at right). Using the brad nailer and ¾-inch nails, attach the shingle to the gable as shown.

12 Add shingles to the left of the center, then to the right, overlapping the ends.

13

14

15

TIP

POSITION THE LOWER SHINGLES ON THE GABLE SO THAT THEIR CURVED EDGES DO NOT EXTEND INTO THE BOOKCASE OPENING. TO MARK A GUIDELINE, STAND THE GABLE ON TOP OF THE CASE AND PLACE A SHINGLE SO IT OVERLAPS JUST THE RIGHT AMOUNT, THEN MARK THE GABLE AT THE UPPER EDGE OF THE SHINGLE. DRAW A LINE THROUGH THIS POINT ACROSS THE WIDTH OF THE GABLE.

13 Position the first shingle for the second row, placing its right edge at the center line so the curve is centered over the two shingles below and overlaps the top of them. Nail the shingle to the gable. Work to the left, then to the right, as you did on the first row.

14 Position the first shingle for the third row, placing it over the center line. Nail it to the gable. Work to the left, then to the right.

15 Attach the shingles for the fourth row. Add the top shingle.

16 Turn the gable right side down and clamp it to your work surface so the shingles extend over the edge of the surface. Using the circular saw, trim the shingles flush with the sloping sides.

16

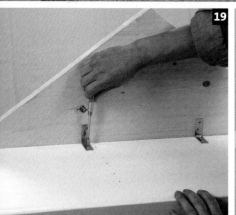

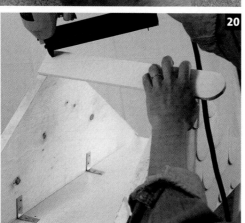

Painting the Pieces

17 Prime the front of the shingled gable, one side of the plain gable, the roof slats (both faces and all edges), the wood brackets, and all the corner guard trim. Paint with the yellow latex paint.

Attaching the Gables

18 On the wrong side of each gable, divide the lower edge into thirds; mark the two points. Attach one arm of a corner bracket at each mark as shown.

19 Place the plain gable on top of the bookcase, flush with the back edge. Screw the other arm of each corner bracket into the top of the case. Do the same with the shingled gable on the front of the shelf.

20 At the peak of the gables, lay a roof slat so its straight end is flush with the back gable. Using the brad nailer and 3/4-inch nails, attach the slat to both gables.

21 Continue nailing slats to the roof, allowing the last one on each side to hang over the end.

Making the Window and Door Frames

22 For each window you'll need four ripped trim pieces for the outside and four ripped trim pieces for the inside. To cut a piece, position the trim in the adjustable miter box so the narrower (ripped) edge is standing up, as shown; make the first 45-degree-angle cut. Make the next cut at a distance equal to the corresponding window opening measurement.

23 Cut a complete set of inside pieces as shown. Repeat to cut an identical set of outside pieces.

24 Run a thin bead of wood glue on the wider edge of one trim piece and attach it to the window opening on the inside of the bookcase.

25 Glue the remaining inside trim pieces.

26 Glue the outside trim pieces.

27 For door trim, cut the inside and outside trim pieces for each side so the lower ends are straight across and flush with the bottom of the door opening; miter the upper ends of the side pieces and both ends of the top trim pieces. Cut the threshold piece from the trim that was not ripped, cutting each end straight across.

28 Glue the wood brackets to the upper corners of the bookcase.

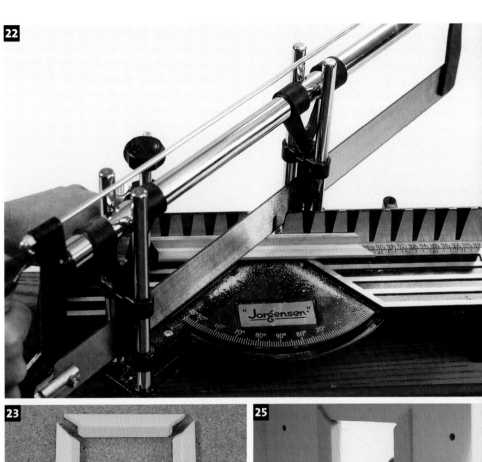

MATERIALS

Five rounds of foam, each 30 inches in diameter and 4 inches thick, available at upholstery shops

3¼ yards of large-check cotton fabric, 54 or 60 inches wide, for the ottoman cover

1- by 12-inch rotary ruler and 6- by 24-inch rotary ruler, available at fabric stores and quilt shops

Fabric scissors

1½ yards of narrow-stripe cotton fabric, 54 or 60 inches wide, for the welt

Thread

3¼ yards of ½-inch cord for the welt

Pins

Spray adhesive

Bonded batting (see the tip at right)

NOTE: Do not prewash fabrics. Washing destroys the fabric's finish, which helps repel stains. Plan to remove and dry-clean the ottoman cover as necessary.

SEWING WORKSHOP

Party Ottoman

IT'S A PLACE TO PERCH, a table for tea, a throne for a princess. This party ottoman "makes" any room it graces, while offering its owner a special place to play. Batting covering the top and sides of the foam form gives it an upholstered look and keeps the cover taut. Easing the cover over the form is a bit of a challenge, so take your time.

FINISHED SIZE 30 inches in diameter, 20 inches tall

Cutting the Pieces

1 For the top, lay one round of foam on the wrong side of the ottoman fabric, 1 inch from two edges. Draw around the foam circle onto the fabric, using a pencil.

2 Using the 1- by 12-inch rotary ruler, mark a ½-inch seam allowance beyond the line you marked in the previous step. Cut out the top on the marked line. Use the top as a pattern to cut out a second circle for the ottoman bottom.

3 For the welt, fold the striped fabric in half diagonally (right or wrong sides together) and press the fold. Carefully cut on the fold to make two large triangular pieces. Using the 6- by 24-inch rotary ruler, measure and mark three 1⅝-inch-wide strips on each triangular piece, starting at the long cut edges, for a total of six strips. Cut the strips.

4 For the side panel, cut two pieces, each 22 inches by the width of the fabric. If your fabric has a large-scale pattern, like this check, cut the pieces so the pattern will match. With right sides together and selvages aligned, stitch the two pieces using a ½-inch seam allowance; backstitch at the beginning and end to secure. Press the seam allowances open.

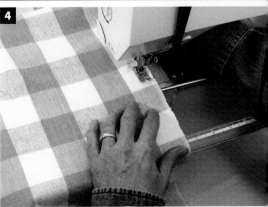

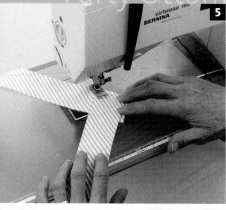

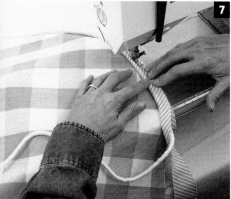

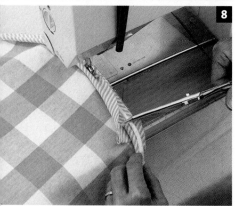

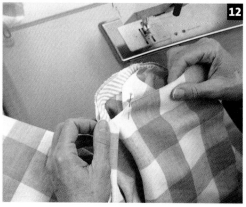

Making and Attaching the Welt

5 With right sides together, overlap the ends of two welt strips at a right angle and match the stripes, as shown; sew diagonally across the corner (see the tip below). Trim the seam allowances to ¼ inch; press open. Repeat with the remaining pieces to make one long strip.

6 Attach the zipper foot to your sewing machine, positioning the foot to the right of the needle.

7 The following technique stitches the welt and attaches it to the ottoman top in one step. With the strip wrong side up, lay the cord in the middle; fold the strip over the cord, encasing it. Lay the ottoman top right side up. Leaving approximately 1½ inches of the strip and cord free, align the raw edges of the welt with the raw edge of the ottoman top. Stitch around the curve, keeping the zipper foot snug against the cord and the raw edges aligned.

8 Stop stitching approximately 4 inches from the start of the welt. Overlap the welt approximately 1½ inches beyond the starting end; cut. Turn in the finishing end of the strip approximately ¾ inch; lay the starting end on top and cut the cord so the ends butt.

9 Wrap the strip over the butted ends and finish sewing the welt to the ottoman top, keeping the zipper foot snug against the cord.

10 Repeat to attach the welt to the ottoman bottom. Set the bottom piece aside.

Stitching the Side Panel

11 With right sides together, position the side panel on the ottoman top several inches away from the overlapped welt. Leaving the first 3 inches of the side panel free, sew the panel to the ottoman top. As you stitch, make sure the zipper foot is snug against the welt underneath.

12 Stop stitching about 3 inches from the free end and take the piece out from under the needle. Bring the ends of the side panel together to determine where to stitch the side seam; pin the spot.

13 Lay the piece on your work surface. Pull the top of the ottoman to one side, then pin the edges of the side panel together. Stitch, starting at the point you pinned in Step 12. Trim the seam allowances to ½ inch and press the seam open.

14 Finish stitching the side panel to the ottoman top.

Adhering the Batting

15 Using the spray adhesive outdoors, spray and layer the five rounds of foam to make the ottoman form.

16 Cut a circle of batting slightly larger than 30 inches in diameter to fit the top of the foam form. Spray the form and adhere the batting circle to it. Trim the batting flush with the sides of the form.

17 Cut a strip of batting that is approximately 25 inches wide and the length of the remainder of the batting.

18 Still working outside, spray the sides of the foam form. Roll the ottoman onto the batting strip. When you reach the start, trim the ends of the batting flush with each other. Trim the excess batting from the top and bottom edges. Slipstitch the side batting to the top batting along the curved edge to keep the pieces from shifting.

Finishing the Ottoman

19 With the ottoman form right side up, ease the cover over the form, working it evenly down the sides. The cover will be taut, but resist the urge to tug on it.

20 Turn the ottoman upside down. Smooth the raw edge of the side panel over the bottom of the form. Pin the ottoman bottom to the side panel, turning under the seam allowances on the bottom piece along the welt stitching. Slipstitch the welted edge of the ottoman bottom to the side panel.

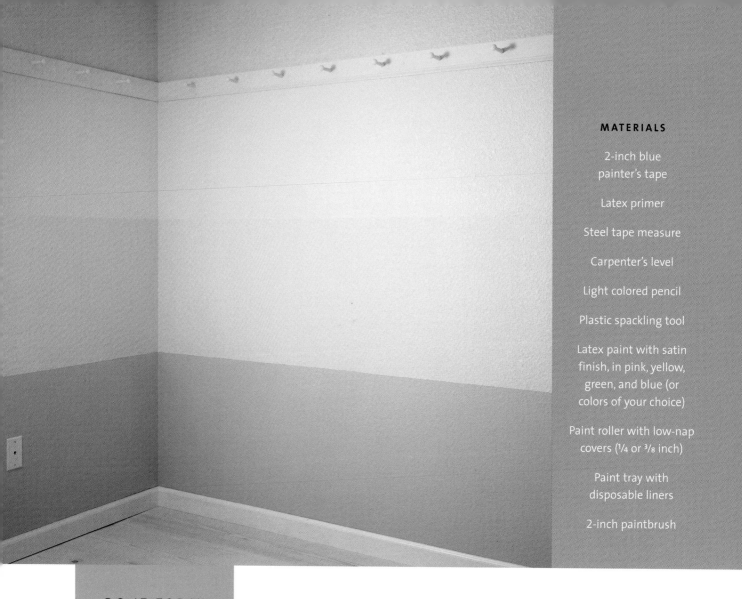

MATERIALS

2-inch blue
painter's tape

Latex primer

Steel tape measure

Carpenter's level

Light colored pencil

Plastic spackling tool

Latex paint with satin
finish, in pink, yellow,
green, and blue (or
colors of your choice)

Paint roller with low-nap
covers (¼ or ⅜ inch)

Paint tray with
disposable liners

2-inch paintbrush

DO IT TODAY

Striped Walls

THIS SUPER-SIMPLE PAINT TREATMENT makes a graphic statement, even when the colors are soft and sweet. You can choose four colors from a multicolored fabric (in this room the valance fabric was the color catalyst) or build a palette based on your child's favorite colors. Whichever approach you take, select colors that have roughly the same value (relative lightness or darkness) and intensity (brightness or dullness). Painter's tape and a carpenter's level are key to achieving crisp, straight lines.

FINISHED SIZE 2-foot-wide stripes

TIP

THESE STRIPES WERE

PAINTED IN A ROOM WITH

A STANDARD 8-FOOT

CEILING. IF YOUR ROOM

HAS A HIGHER CEILING,

DIVIDE THE HEIGHT BY 4

TO ARRIVE AT THE WIDTH

OF THE STRIPES.

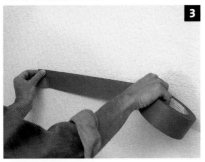

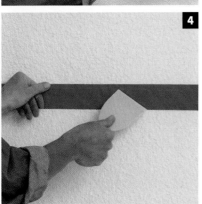

1 Using blue painter's tape, tape the baseboards, window frames, and ceiling line; prime the walls if necessary. Leave the tape in place. On each wall, measure and lightly mark points at 2-foot vertical intervals.

2 Using the carpenter's level and the colored pencil, lightly join the points to mark three horizontal lines on each wall.

3 In preparation for painting the first and third stripes from the top (pink and yellow on these walls), tape below the first line, above the second line, and below the third line.

4 Press down the edges of the tape with the spackling tool. If your walls are textured, also use your fingers to adhere the tape along the edges to be painted.

5 Using the paint roller, paint the first stripe pink, overlapping the tape. Paint the third stripe yellow.

6 Paint the corners and ceiling line using the brush.

7 When the paint is dry, remove the tape below the pink stripe; above the yellow stripe, as shown; and below the yellow stripe.

8 Retape the walls, placing tape over the bottom edge of the pink stripe; over the top edge of the yellow stripe, as shown; and over the bottom edge of the yellow stripe.

9 Press down the edges of the tape. Paint the second stripe green and the fourth stripe blue. Paint the corners and the bottom edge using the brush. When the paint is dry, remove the tape.

And Everything
Nice

Pocket Panel

Sheer fabric allows treasures and toys in this pocketed wall hanging to be seen. The pockets were adhered with iron-on fusible tape. The loops were spaced to correspond to the peg placement.

Plank Floor

TOP RIGHT: One-by-twelve pine planking, whitewashed with dilute latex paint and sealed with polyurethane, makes a clean-looking (and inexpensive) floor covering.

Painted Knobs

BOTTOM RIGHT: Plain knobs on a simple pine dresser were treated to the same colors as the wall. The dresser front was whitewashed to match the floors, and the top was painted white to match the bed frame and bookcases.

Bib Pillows

BELOW: Denim pockets left over from the valance (see page 124) decorate pillows made from the valance fabric and trimmed with ottoman welt.

Index

Numbers in **boldface** refer to additional photographs.

Buttons attach a plaid sheet to the cotton duck spread and add a bit of color to the bedding. See "Shared Space," page 30.